EXPLORE
NATIVE AMERICAN CULTURES!

Anita Yasuda
Illustrated by Jennifer K. Keller

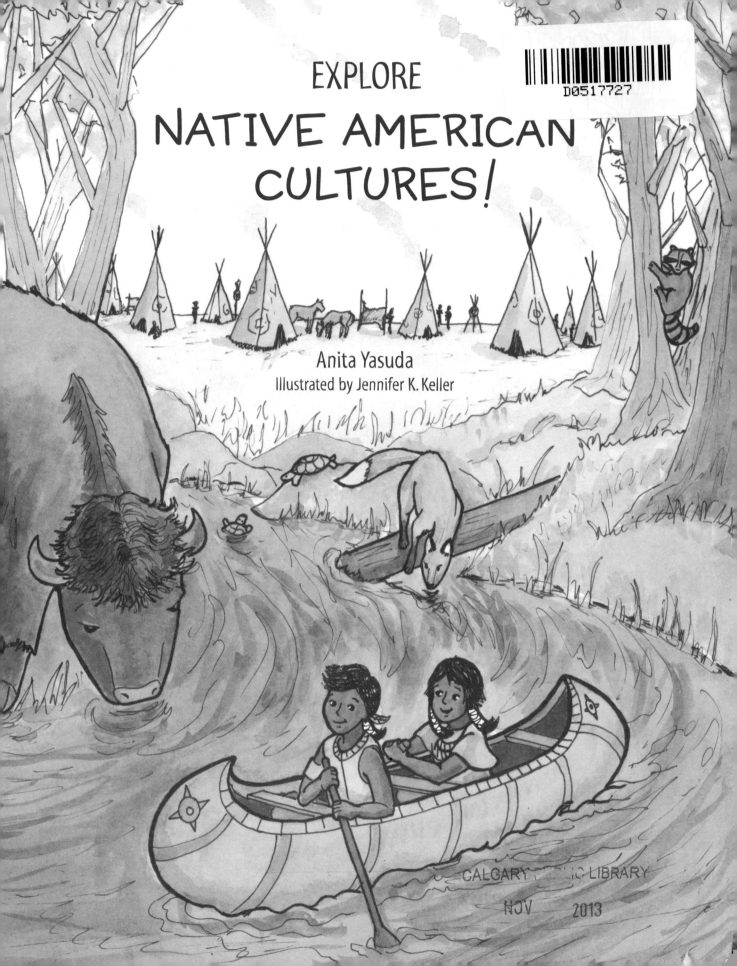

Newest titles in the **Explore Your World!** Series

Nomad Press
A division of Nomad Communications
10 9 8 7 6 5 4 3 2 1

Manufactured by Thomson-Shore, Dexter, MI (USA)
March 2013, RMA587433
ISBN: 978-1-61930-160-3

Illustrations by Jennifer K. Keller
Educational Consultant, Marla Conn

Questions regarding the ordering of this book should be addressed to
Independent Publishers Group
814 N. Franklin St.
Chicago, IL 60610
www.ipgbook.com

Nomad Press
2456 Christian St.
White River Junction, VT 05001
www.nomadpress.net

Nomad Press is committed to preserving ancient forests and natural resources. We elected to print *Explore Native American Cultures!* on 30% post consumer recycled paper, processed chlorine free. **As a result, for this printing, we have saved:**

- 10 Trees (40' tall and 6-8" diameter)
- 4,286 Gallons of Wastewater
- 4 Million BTU's of Total Energy
- 286 Pounds of Solid Waste
- 790 Pounds of Greenhouse Gases

Nomad Press made this paper choice because our printer, Thomson-Shore, Inc., is a member of Green Press Initiative, a nonprofit program dedicated to supporting authors, publishers, and suppliers in their efforts to reduce their use of fiber obtained from endangered forests. For more information, **visit www.greenpressinitiative.org.**

Environmental impact estimates were made using the Environmental Defense Paper Calculator. For more information visit: www.papercalculator.org.

CONTENTS

Timeline

Pre-European Period

THE PALEO-INDIAN PERIOD: 20,000 BCE–8000 BCE
It is believed that the ancestors of the Native Americans
came to North America during this period.

8000 BCE: Large North American animals such as
the woolly mammoth begin to die, perhaps due to
a change in the climate. This is called the Great Animal
Die-Off.

THE ARCHAIC PERIOD: 8000 BCE–3500 BCE
People hunted and gathered their food.
They did not grow their own food or live in
permanent year-round settlements.

5000 BCE: Native Americans start growing
maize, a type of corn.

3500 BCE: Native Americans grow squash
and beans.

THE FORMATIVE PERIOD: 3500 BCE–1600 CE
There is a shift from moving around to hunt and
gather food to farming and living in more
permanent settlements. Native American
cultures flourishes. Pottery is being made.

Timeline

European Colonization Period

1400–1500: European explorers arrive in North America.

1621: The Pilgrims and the Native Americans share a feast that we celebrate today as Thanksgiving.

1830: President Andrew Jackson signs the Indian Removal Act.

1838: 15,000 Cherokees are forced to relocate to Oklahoma. Because so many die on the trip, the walk becomes known as the Trail of Tears.

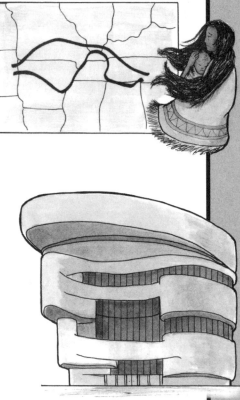

1876: At the Battle of Little Bighorn, Sitting Bull and Crazy Horse defeat Lt. Colonel George Custer.

1964: Tribal Law is restored on reservations with the passing of the Civil Rights Act.

1978: The passing of the American Indian Religious Freedom Act makes Native American religious practices legal again.

1996: November is declared National American Indian Heritage Month by President Bill Clinton.

2004: The National Museum of the American Indian opens in Washington, D.C.

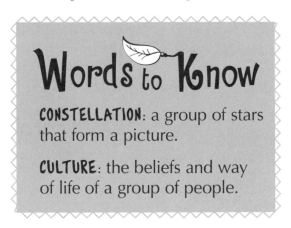

INTRODUCTION

Have you ever played lacrosse or paddled a kayak? Or looked in the night sky at the **CONSTELLATION** Great Bear? Maybe you've heard stories of Earth resting on the back of a giant turtle or the great leader Hiawatha. Guess what? These are all part of Native American **CULTURE**.

Words to Know

CONSTELLATION: a group of stars that form a picture.

CULTURE: the beliefs and way of life of a group of people.

Who are Native Americans? Where did they come from? Native Americans are different groups of people who have lived in the Americas for thousands of years. In this book, you'll explore the fascinating life and culture of many different groups of Native Americans in North America.

1

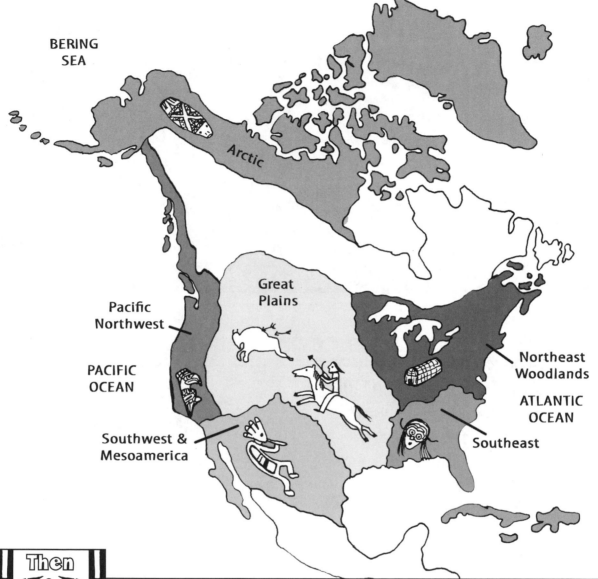

BERING SEA

Arctic

Great Plains

Pacific Northwest

PACIFIC OCEAN

Southwest & Mesoamerica

Northeast Woodlands

ATLANTIC OCEAN

Southeast

Then & Now

Then – In 1492, explorer Christopher Columbus sailed from Spain across the Atlantic Ocean looking for a route to India to **TRADE** for spices. When he landed in North America, he thought that he was in India, so he named the people he met Indians.

Now – Today, these native people are called Native Americans, First Nations, aboriginal people, or by their tribal name.

How did Native Americans live 400 years ago, around the time people arrived in North America from Europe? What is life like now for Native American people? This book divides North America into six Native American cultural areas:

* Northeast Woodlands
* Southeast
* Southwest and **MESOAMERICA**
* **GREAT PLAINS**
* Pacific Northwest
* **ARCTIC**

You'll learn how Native Americans used the **NATURAL RESOURCES** around them for food, shelter, and clothing. In *Explore Native American Cultures!* you'll meet some amazing people like Sacagawea, Sequoyah, and Geronimo. While reading about the challenges Native Americans faced, you'll be amazed at what they were able to invent and build long ago.

By the end of this book you'll be making a calendar of pictures, creating a home from sticks and leaves, and using a few words in Native American sign language. There will be lots of fun facts, too. So get ready to head across North America as you *Explore Native American Cultures!*

Words to Know

TRADE: to exchange goods for other goods or money.

MESOAMERICA: the region that includes parts of Mexico and Central America.

GREAT PLAINS: a flat area of land that is covered with grass in the middle of North America.

ARCTIC: the region in the far north around the North Pole.

NATURAL RESOURCE: something found in nature that is useful to humans, such as water to drink, trees to burn and build with, and fish to eat.

Where Did Native Americans Come From?

The last **ICE AGE** began 80,000 years ago and ended 12,000 years ago. **GLACIERS** up to 2 miles thick covered the earth (3 kilometers).

With so much water trapped in ice, the level of the oceans dropped. Land that was usually under the water was above the surface. One important sea passage that dried up was the **BERING STRAIT**. This created a temporary **LAND BRIDGE** that was 1,242 miles wide (2,000 kilometers).

Words to Know

ICE AGE: a period of time when ice covers a large part of the earth.

GLACIER: a huge sheet of ice and snow.

BERING STRAIT: a narrow sea passage between Russia in Asia and Alaska in North America.

LAND BRIDGE: a connection between two land masses that allows humans and animals to settle in new areas.

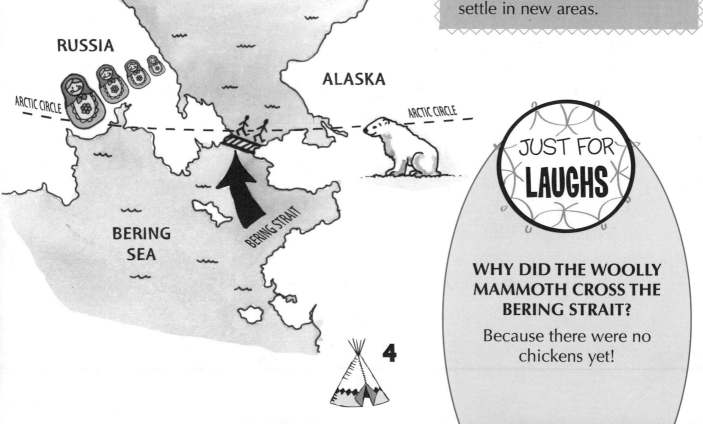

RUSSIA

ALASKA

ARCTIC CIRCLE

ARCTIC CIRCLE

BERING STRAIT

BERING SEA

4

JUST FOR LAUGHS

WHY DID THE WOOLLY MAMMOTH CROSS THE BERING STRAIT?

Because there were no chickens yet!

Around 10,000 years ago, huge ice-age animals like the woolly mammoth began to die and many plants changed. This was probably due to climate change at the end of the Ice Age.

WOW!

Most scientists think hunters from Asia crossed this land bridge into North America. **ARCHAEOLOGISTS** have found spear heads over 13,000 years old. The hunters were probably following herds of animals like the woolly mammoth and musk ox, and used the spear heads to kill them. These people were the **ANCESTORS** of Native Americans. Over hundreds of years, they moved south from Alaska, spreading across the Americas.

Words to Know

ARCHAEOLOGIST: a scientist who studies ancient people and their cultures by looking at what they left behind.

ANCESTOR: someone from your family or culture who lived before you.

MIGRATE: to move from one place to another when seasons change.

There are some scientists who believe that the ancestors of the Native Americans sailed across the Pacific Ocean on boats from Asia and Polynesia. They may have sailed from island to island until they reached North and South America. Maybe you will be the archaeologist who discovers an ancient boat that proves this happened!

Then & Now

Then – Land animals including the musk ox and the woolly mammoth journeyed across the Bering Land Bridge.

Now – Over 170 species of birds from 6 continents **MIGRATE** to the Bering Land Bridge National Preserve.

MAKE YOUR OWN

RELIEF MAP OF NATIVE AMERICAN REGIONS

This three-dimensional map will give you an understanding of some of the lands where Native American groups lived. The map includes the 48 continental states of the United States, not including Alaska and Hawaii. **This map is not edible.**

1 Print the map of the United States showing the Native American regions. Cut out the map and set it to one side.

2 Place the salt and flour in a bowl. Add the cream of tartar and enough water to make a thick dough. Mix the dough with your hands until it is smooth. You can add more water if it is too thick, or more flour if it is too thin.

3 Start making your map by placing the dough on the cardboard. Use your hands to press it into a large rectangle. Spread the dough out almost to the edges.

4 Press the paper map over the salt dough. Trim off the excess dough with a butter knife. You should follow the outline of the paper map all the way around.

SUPPLIES

- ⊙ map of the United States with Native American regions *(www.nomadpress.net/resources)*
- ⊙ scissors
- ⊙ 2 cups of salt (500 grams)
- ⊙ 2 cups of flour (250 grams)
- ⊙ large bowl
- ⊙ 2 tablespoons cream of tartar
- ⊙ water
- ⊙ piece of cardboard about 12 by 15 inches (30 by 38 centimeters)
- ⊙ butter knife
- ⊙ paint and paintbrush, 5 different colors
- ⊙ paper and pen
- ⊙ tape
- ⊙ toothpicks

6

5 Peel off the paper map and set it to one side. Use leftover dough to build up mountain ranges, and make indentations in the dough for major rivers and lakes.

6 Use a paintbrush and paint each Native American region a different color. Write the name of each region on a piece of paper. Cut them out and tape each to a toothpick. Push the toothpicks into the correct regions on your map. Let your map dry.

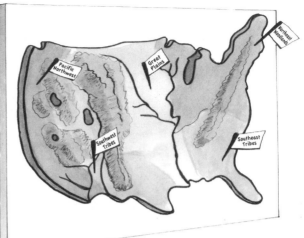

Words to Know

GENERATION: all the people born around the same time.

Native American Beliefs

Most Native Americans believe their people have always lived in North America. These beliefs passed from one **GENERATION** to the next in songs and stories. Hopi stories speak of a spiritual being called Spider Woman who created life through the song of creation. The Cherokee believe a small water beetle helped to form Earth from mud. The Haida of the West Coast give the Raven credit for providing everything they needed to live, from the sun and moon to water and the trees.

7

THE NORTHEAST WOODLANDS

The Northeast Woodlands stretched from the Atlantic coast to the Great Plains and from the Great Lakes south toward the Gulf of Mexico. Great forests covered the land. A huge variety of plants, birds, and animals lived in its mountains, valleys, lakes, and rivers.

Spring and fall were short seasons, sandwiched between cold winters and warm summers. This area was home to two major language groups, the Iroquois and the Algonquin.

The Iroquois called themselves *Haudenosaunee* (pronounced hoe-dee-no-SHOW-nee), which means "people of the **LONGHOUSE**." The Algonquin called themselves *Anishinabe* (a-ni-shi-NA-bay), meaning "original people." Within each group were several **TRIBES** with similar **CUSTOMS**. They didn't always get along and sometimes fought each other.

Iroquois Confederacy

Around 1570, several Iroquois tribes decided to work together. According to Iroquois history, a peacemaker had help from a man named **HIAWATHA**. They convinced the Seneca, Cayuga, Onondaga, Oneida, and Mohawk tribes to accept the **GREAT LAW OF PEACE**. Hiawatha told them that while one arrow can be broken easily, five arrows bound together cannot. The five tribes formed a council of tribal leaders called the Iroquois Confederacy.

Words to Know

LONGHOUSE: a long home that housed several Iroquois families.

TRIBE: a large group of people with common ancestors and customs.

CUSTOMS: traditions or ways of doing things, such as dress, food, or holidays.

HIAWATHA: the leader and founder of the Iroquois Confederacy.

GREAT LAW OF PEACE: the spoken rules that bound the Iroquois tribes together.

Benjamin Franklin was greatly impressed by the Iroquois Confederacy. He wrote that if the Iroquois were able to come together, then the 13 American colonies should be able to make a similar agreement. WOW!

Tadodaho

Tadodaho, Chief of the Onondaga, did not join the Iroquois Confederacy right away. According to stories, he was a sorcerer with a twisted body and hair crawling in snakes! Until Tadodaho joined the group, there could be no true peace. When the peacemaker held a ceremony to straighten Chief Tadodaho's body and rid his hair of snakes, Tadodaho allowed the Onondaga to join the Iroquois Confederacy. Tadodaho became the fire keeper, or chairman of the council.

The Tuscarora tribe joined in the 1700s, and the confederacy became a group of six. Each tribe had a **REPRESENTATIVE**. Before a decision could be made final, all the representatives had to agree.

Words to Know

REPRESENTATIVE: a single person who speaks for the wishes of a group.

WAMPUM: shell beads used in ceremonies or to trade.

WAMPUM belts tell some of the story of the Iroquois Confederacy using strings of colored beads. The strings were woven into patterns that recorded important events. They were also used to send messages between communities. Wampum belts were never used as clothing. The Hiawatha Belt is made of 892 white and 5,682 purple wampum beads. It shows the five original members of the Iroquois Confederacy as squares on either side of a tree. The tree is the Onondaga tribe, whose home is where the five tribes buried their weapons to make peace.

Welcome to My Home

The Iroquois built villages in forest clearings or by rivers. They built **PALISADES**, or wooden fences, around their villages as protection from attack and harsh winter storms. Inside the palisades, longhouses could be 120 feet long (36 meters). Some were 300 feet long (91 meters), longer than a football field.

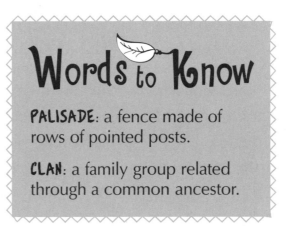

Words to Know

PALISADE: a fence made of rows of pointed posts.

CLAN: a family group related through a common ancestor.

Through the cold winter months, a fire pit kept the longhouse warm. Small holes in the roof let smoke out and were the only source of light since longhouses had no windows.

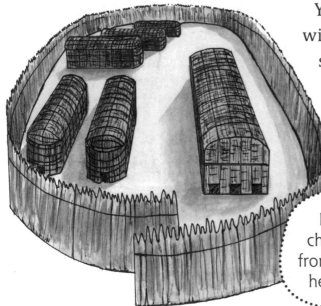

You might think sharing a bedroom with your sibling is tough. Imagine sharing your home with 60 people! Large **CLANS** shared one longhouse. Within the longhouse each family had its own space to sleep, eat, and work.

Native Americans discovered chewing gum! They chewed on sap from spruce trees to help cure headaches and other illness.

WOW!

The **WIGWAM** was another style of home found in the Northeast Woodlands. It was used by the Algonquin-speaking neighbors of the Iroquois. Some wigwams were only big enough for two people and others could fit up to eight family members.

Men built wigwams by bending young saplings or branches and tying them together. They covered the frame with strips of bark or cattail mats. Unlike at your home, a wigwam's door was a flap made of animal skin.

By Land and Water

The main way to travel in the Northeast Woodlands was on foot. But this was not fast or easy, especially when it snowed. So people invented a shoe to help them walk on the snow. We call this a **SNOWSHOE**. Snowshoes were made with a wood frame and woven strips of **HIDE** called **RAWHIDE**. They came in different shapes. Swallowtails were long and pointed and bear paws were oval shaped.

Words to Know

WIGWAM: the rounded or rectangular homes of the Algonquin tribes. Cone-shaped wigwams are different from tipis mainly because they are fixed and not portable.

SNOWSHOE: a shoe like a tennis racket worn on each foot for walking in deep snow.

HIDE: an animal skin.

RAWHIDE: animal skin that has not been turned into leather.

How did hunters carry food home in deep snow? By pulling a **TOBOGGAN** made from planks of wood tied together with rawhide. The toboggan glided smoothly over the snow. Sometimes teams of dogs pulled the sleds, which could be over 10 feet long (3 meters).

Words to Know

TOBOGGAN: a long, narrow sled.

CANOE: a narrow boat with pointy ends.

PORTAGE: to carry a boat over land.

Then & Now

Then – Native American people used toboggans to move goods from one place to another.

Now – People race toboggan-style sleds in the Olympic sports of bobsledding and luge.

When the ice melted on rivers and lakes, people traveled by **CANOE** to hunt, fish, and trade. Men made dugout canoes by carving out the trunk of a large tree. They were heavy and mostly used on large lakes. A finished canoe held up to 40 people! Smaller and lighter canoes were made from spruce or cedar frames covered with sheets of birchbark. Birchbark canoes were made in the summer when it was easier to peel large sheets of bark from trees. The seams were sealed with spruce gum. These canoes were so light they could be **PORTAGED** between lakes and rivers.

Clothing

Making deerskin clothes was a skill mothers passed down to their daughters. It was hard work to clean and **TAN** animal skins to make them soft enough to cut.

Men wore **BREECHCLOTHS** or leather **APRONS** with deerskin leggings. Women wore dresses or wrap-around skirts with leggings similar to the men. In cold weather, everyone wore beaver fur robes to stay warm and dry. You could tell which clan people belonged to by the designs on their soft-soled leather **MOCCASINS**.

Words to Know

TANNING: the process of turning an animal skin into leather by soaking it in liquid.

BREECHCLOTH: a single piece of cloth wrapped around the hips.

APRON: a panel worn over the front and back of a belt.

MOCCASIN: a shoe made from soft leather.

Food

Woodland people farmed, hunted, and gathered food from forests and waterways. Men hunted deer and moose and trapped smaller animals. They used spears, nets, and hooks made of bone to catch fish like herring or trout. They roasted or dried fish to be stored and eaten later.

Women gathered roots, nuts, berries, and fruit. They grew corn, beans, and squash in their gardens. These plants were known as "the three sisters" because they helped each other. The beans fertilized the soil. The cornstalks were poles on which the beans grew. The squash leaves shaded the ground and kept the soil from drying out too quickly. Together, these vegetables made a popular dish that is still called by its Algonquin name—succotash.

Words to Know

SAP: the liquid that flows in maple trees and other plants.

Maple Sugaring

When winter days began to warm up, it was time for maple syrup! Everyone helped collect **SAP**. Maple trees were tapped with a wooden spike and birchbark buckets collected the dripping sap. When the buckets were full, the watery liquid was poured into huge containers made of moosehide or wood and boiled until it was the thick syrup we know today as maple syrup. Do you like syrup on your pancakes? Native Americans used it to sweeten grains, teas, fruits, and vegetables.

Beliefs and Festivals

The people of the Northern Woodlands believed in a Great Spirit who made the earth and everything on it. Some spirits were good but others brought poor harvests and sickness. The Iroquois held ceremonies during the year to give thanks to the spirits and to ask for their help.

Words to Know

PILGRIMS: people who came from England in the 1620s to settle in Massachusetts.

CROP: plants grown for food and other uses.

The Midwinter Ceremony marked the beginning of the New Year. It was held in January or February when the stars of the Big Dipper and Little Dipper constellations appeared overhead. During the festival people stirred the ashes of the fire to represent new soil for the planting season and as a way of thanking the spirits.

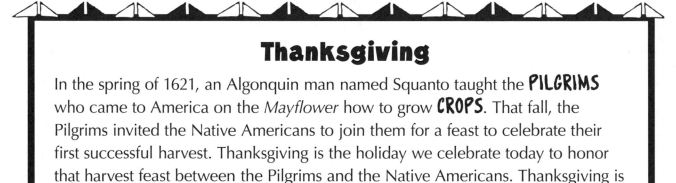

Thanksgiving

In the spring of 1621, an Algonquin man named Squanto taught the **PILGRIMS** who came to America on the *Mayflower* how to grow **CROPS**. That fall, the Pilgrims invited the Native Americans to join them for a feast to celebrate their first successful harvest. Thanksgiving is the holiday we celebrate today to honor that harvest feast between the Pilgrims and the Native Americans. Thanksgiving is celebrated on the fourth Thursday of November in the United States and on the second Monday of October in Canada.

Let's Play!

Girls learned to weave baskets, make clothes, and gather food. Boys learned to trap animals and make tools like bows and arrows. But there was still time for fun. Young children played with dolls and rolled birchbark hoops.

Grownups played games too! In winter, they played Snow Snake. Players carved a long stick to look like a snake and decorated it with snakeskin and feathers. They dragged a log through the snow to make a path. Players held the narrower end of their stick and threw it down the slippery path. The stick that went farthest down the path was the winner.

Lacrosse, known to the Iroquois as *baggataway*, is a 500-year-old sport. Each player had a stick made from a young sapling that was bent at the end to form a loop. When some French people saw the stick it reminded them of a cross and they named it la crosse. Lacrosse was played by as many as 100 or even 1,000 men on fields that stretched for miles between villages. A game could last for days.

WOW!

Where Are We Now?

Today, most people with Algonquin and Iroquois ancestors live in cities and towns in modern homes. Some Algonquin still live on **RESERVATIONS** in Canada, and some Iroquois live on reservations in Canada, New York, and Wisconsin.

While some Algonquin and Iroquois people still farm, others are lawyers, teachers, doctors, nurses, business people, artists, and construction workers. The Iroquois are known to be good ironworkers and have worked on some of the country's most famous structures, including the Empire State Building in New York and the Golden Gate Bridge in San Francisco.

Words to Know

RESERVATION: land owned by the United States but set aside for Native American tribes. There are about 326 Indian reservations in the United States.

ARCHITECTURE: the style or look of a building.

HERITAGE: the art, buildings, traditions, and beliefs that are important to the world's history.

COMMUNITY: a group of people who live in the same area.

Native American Tech

Wampum is still made today and it inspires modern **ARCHITECTURE**. In 1991 at Cornell University, a residence was built to celebrate Native American culture and **HERITAGE**. It uses designs found on the Hiawatha Belt in a series of window frames, glass, and shingles. The residence is called Akwe:kon (pronounced uh-gway-go), an Iroquois word that means "all of us." The name reflects a spirit of **COMMUNITY** and a purpose to preserve and share the heritage of Native Americans.

IROQUOIS TURTLE SHELL RATTLE

Rattles were made from animal skin, wood, gourds, and shells. The Iroquois played turtle shell rattles by beating them on the edge of longhouse benches. Research and investigate different turtle shell patterns on the Internet. Find one you like for your project. **Ask an adult to supervise while you are on the Internet.**

1 Take the paper bag and a crayon. Color and add turtle shell patterns to it.

2 Blow air into the bag to make it puff out. Pour in the corn or pebbles.

3 Place the stick into the open end of the bag, leaving enough poking out the end to make a handle. Secure the end of the bag and the stick handle with tape.

4 Wrap twine or string around the tape. Glue feathers, beads, and raffia to the string. The rafia represents horsehair. Wrap the rafia around the top of the handle. Now your instrument is ready to play.

SUPPLIES

- ⊙ small brown paper bag
- ⊙ brown crayon
- ⊙ corn or pebbles
- ⊙ stick
- ⊙ tape
- ⊙ twine or string
- ⊙ glue
- ⊙ feathers, beads, and raffia

An important part of the Iroquois Midwinter Ceremony was dream sharing. People shared their dreams so that others could tell them what the dreams meant.

WOW!

19

MAKE YOUR OWN

LONGHOUSE

The Iroquois men built their longhouses in the spring when the trees were young and flexible. Longhouses were large enough for 20 or more families to live in. Native Americans used materials that they found in nature. They believed that nothing should go to waste. Build a longhouse using as many natural resources as you can find, including dried weeds, straw, and twigs.

1 Turn your shoebox upside down. Cut out a rectangle at either end of your box for the doors.

2 Bend your construction paper to form the domed roof and tape it to the shoebox.

3 Cut three equally spaced squares along the center of the roof.

4 Paint the box brown and let it dry. Cut pieces of brown, white, and green tissue paper for the roof shingles. Glue these into place.

5 Glue the dried weeds, straw, and twigs onto the sides of your box.

6 Cut out pieces of brown felt for the doors and attach with glue.

SUPPLIES

- shoebox without a lid
- scissors
- brown construction paper
- tape
- brown paint
- paint brush
- brown, white, and green tissue paper
- glue
- dried weeds, straw, twigs, and other natural resources
- brown felt

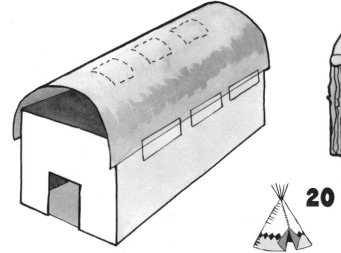
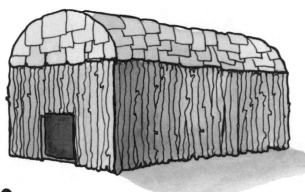

20

MAKE YOUR OWN

WAMPUM BELT

Wampum belt designs recorded important events and agreements between tribes. They are still being made today. In this project, you will create a wampum design of your own. **Ask an adult to supervise while you are on the Internet.**

1 Cut a cardboard rectangle about 2½ by 8 inches (6 by 20 centimeters). Use the hole punch to make three holes at each end of the rectangle.

2 With an adult's help, look at pictures of wampum belts. Use the markers to draw a design in colors you will cover with your beads.

3 Sort your beads into the small paper cups by color.

4 Brush glue over one section of your cardboard at a time. Apply the beads to match the design. Then work section by section until you are done. Allow it to dry fully.

5 Tie string or yarn to each hole. The strings should reach around your waist. You can wear your belt or hang it as a decoration.

SUPPLIES

- ⊙ cardboard
- ⊙ scissors
- ⊙ hole punch
- ⊙ Internet access to research pictures of wampum belts
- ⊙ colored markers
- ⊙ small colored crafting beads
- ⊙ small paper cups
- ⊙ white glue
- ⊙ small paint brush
- ⊙ string or yarn

The Iroquois Confederacy peace ceremony was one of the earliest known ceremonies in which war weapons were actually buried. It is probably where the phrase "bury the hatchet" came from. We use the phrase today to mean "to make peace."

BIRCHBARK CANOE

The largest birchbark canoe in the world is 3 feet high by 36 feet long (1 by 11 meters). It was created for the National Museum of Canada in 1956.

1 Peel the wrapper off the crayon. Take the craft paper and crayon and find a tree to make your bark rubbing. Place the paper on the bark and gently rub the crayon over the paper.

2 Fold the paper lengthwise. Draw a smile on the fold of the paper. This will be your canoe template. Cut out the canoe shape.

3 Thread the needle and sew the ends of the canoe together using an over stitch. You could glue the ends if you prefer. Glue the toothpicks across the canoe for seats.

4 Rub paraffin wax over the canoe to make it waterproof.

SUPPLIES

- ⊙ white crayon
- ⊙ brown craft paper
- ⊙ pencil
- ⊙ scissors
- ⊙ black thread
- ⊙ needle
- ⊙ toothpicks
- ⊙ white glue
- ⊙ paraffin wax

People today put boats in winter storage and so did the Native Americans. They placed rocks in their canoes to sink them to the bottom of a lake. This protected the wood from freezing and thawing over and over each winter. In the spring men would dive into the water and remove the rocks.

WOW!

THE SOUTHEAST

The Southeast is a land of forests, swamps, and the oldest mountain range in North America. The Appalachian Mountains cover a wide area of land in the United States from the Atlantic Ocean to east of the Mississippi River.

Summers in the Southeast are hot and winters are mild. The Native people who called the Southeast home—Cherokee, Chickasaw, Choctaw, Creek (Muscogee), and Seminole—could spend most of their time outdoors. Tribes inland worked together to farm and hunt. Atlantic coastal tribes were skilled at fishing. After the Europeans arrived, tribes began raising **LIVESTOCK**.

23

Communities and Homes

The Seminoles lived in Florida's swamps. They formed as a group of tribes that joined together for protection. The tribes came from what are now the states of Georgia, Alabama, Mississippi, and Florida.

A Seminole **THATCHED** hut known as a **CHICKEE** sat on stilts high above the swampy waters. This prevented the hut from sinking into the mud and kept out alligators and other wildlife. Chickee means "home" in Miccosukee, a Seminole language. A chickee could be built in one day from split logs and palmetto leaves.

Words to Know

LIVESTOCK: animals raised for food and other uses.

THATCH: straw or leaves used as a roof.

CHICKEE: a Seminole home built with plant materials in the swamps of Florida.

Swampy land is not good for growing crops, so Seminoles were on the move hunting and harvesting. When Seminoles were away from their villages, anyone could come along and sleep in an empty chickee. There were no doors and no walls! A small Seminole village might have just two chickees, while a larger village would have between 10 and 12.

To the north, the Cherokee lived in villages of 30 to 60 homes throughout the Appalachian Mountains. By the 1600s, the Cherokee were the most powerful tribe of the Southeast. The Cherokee wove branches and vines together to build strong thatched homes called **ASI** that looked like upside-down baskets. This style of construction is called wattle and daub. The woven branches were the wattle and the mud that covered them was the daub. Part of the asi was underground. This part of the house stayed warmer in the winter and its dirt floor was cool in summer.

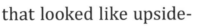

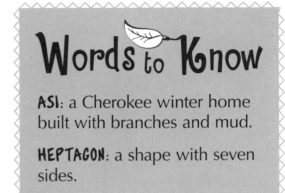

Words to Know

ASI: a Cherokee winter home built with branches and mud.

HEPTAGON: a shape with seven sides.

Cherokee homes were built around a central square used for ceremonies, and an open-air council house used for meetings. Council houses were **HEPTAGONAL** to represent the seven Cherokee clans: Bird, Paint, Deer, Wolf, Blue, Long Hair, and Wild Potato. All tribal members had a say in how they wanted their community to work, and people could go to the council house to speak up.

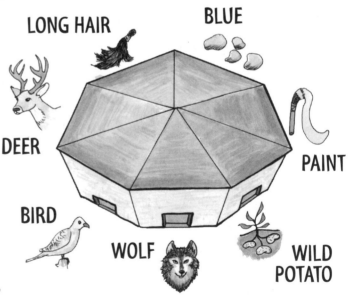

LONG HAIR
BLUE
DEER
PAINT
BIRD
WOLF
WILD POTATO

While many Creeks joined the Seminoles, some stayed in areas that are Georgia and Alabama today. They had red and white villages. A red village was where war leaders lived and where **WARRIORS** came to learn to fight. White villages were peaceful places where no one could be attacked. People living in a white village agreed to live peacefully. Those who couldn't resolve a problem went to a red village until they worked out their differences.

Words to Know

WARRIOR: a brave fighter.

Then – Many North American places took names that Native Americans first used.

NOW – **These names are still used today. They include the names of states of Ohio, Idaho, and Connecticut.**

Creek villages were built around a central plaza and protected by a palisade. A large round building for special ceremonies held all 400 to 500 people from the village. People had winter houses like the wattle and daub homes of the Cherokee and open-air summer houses in the same village. Most villages had a ball field with benches for people to watch games.

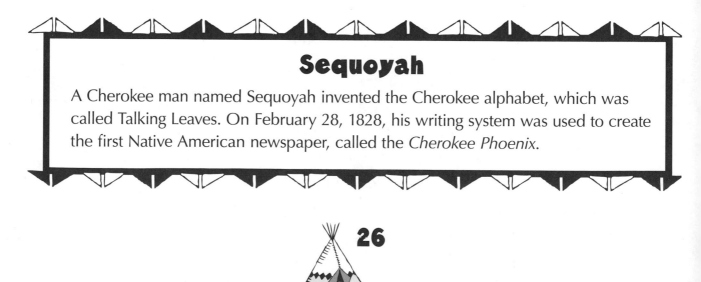

Sequoyah

A Cherokee man named Sequoyah invented the Cherokee alphabet, which was called Talking Leaves. On February 28, 1828, his writing system was used to create the first Native American newspaper, called the *Cherokee Phoenix*.

Food

A family ate what they could hunt, gather, and grow. The women searched for wild plants and roots in the forests. The men caught fish using traps, nets, and spears and hunted deer, turkey, and bear. Nothing was wasted. They turned skins into clothes, turkey feathers into arrows, and fish bones into arrowheads.

Words to Know

FERTILE: land that is good for growing crops.

Tribes living in **FERTILE** regions grew crops of corn, pumpkins, beans, and squash. They worked the soil by hand with tools made from bone, stone, or shells. Imagine how many blisters you'd have on your hands if you had to work through a field over a mile long (1.6 kilometers)! By the end of the 1700s, Creek women had plows and axes to help ease the work.

JUST FOR LAUGHS

WHAT HAS HUNDREDS OF EARS BUT CAN'T HEAR A THING?

A crop of corn!

Families always dried some of their crops to store them for the winter. A hot soup called *sofki* was a popular dish made from stewed dried corn, which the Seminole still enjoy today.

Clothing

In the warm climate of the Southeast, people wanted clothes that would keep them cool. Men wore a breechcloth and women wore knee-length animal-skin skirts. Very young children didn't wear anything at all. Both men and women wore moccasins and capes of fur wrapped around their shoulders when the weather got cold. Once tribes began trading with the Europeans, their styles changed. Cherokee men started wrapping their heads in turbans and Cherokee women made skirts and aprons from CALICO with designs of flowers and vines.

Words to Know

CALICO: a cotton fabric.

TUNIC: a long, loose-fitting shirt.

Farther south in Florida, Seminole women wore skirts woven from tree moss and palmetto leaves. Clothing changed when the Seminoles began trading with the Spanish for cotton cloth. Men wore colorful TUNICS and women sewed brightly colored strips of cloth together to make long patchwork skirts and short capes that showed off their artistic talents. This sewing technique is called Seminole patchwork.

How did Native Americans make clothes with no scissors or sewing machines? They cut animal skin with tools made from shells or flint and used needles made from animal bone or horn to stitch the skins together. Thread was made from **SINEW**.

WOW!

A Seminole woman wore so many strands of beads that they covered her neck all the way up to her ears! Jewelry was an important part of Seminole dress. A girl received her first necklace at **PUBERTY** and another was added every year. At middle age, women began giving away their necklaces one by one until only their first necklace was left.

Words to Know

SINEW: a strong band of animal tissue that connects muscles to bones.

PUBERTY: the stage of development when a child's body starts to change into an adult body.

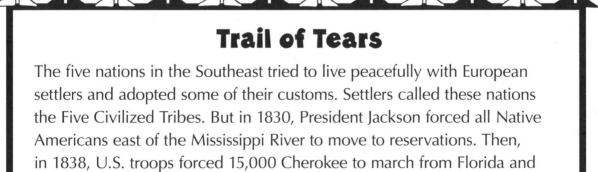

Trail of Tears

The five nations in the Southeast tried to live peacefully with European settlers and adopted some of their customs. Settlers called these nations the Five Civilized Tribes. But in 1830, President Jackson forced all Native Americans east of the Mississippi River to move to reservations. Then, in 1838, U.S. troops forced 15,000 Cherokee to march from Florida and Georgia to Oklahoma. Along the way, 4,000 people died. The Cherokee named the journey the Trail of Tears.

Games

Life was hard, but there was always time for fun and games. Native Americans in the Southeast liked games that tested a warrior's strength or speed. In stickball, players held a stick with a net at one end, similar to today's lacrosse sticks. The deerskin balls were stuffed with deer or squirrel hair. Players had to scoop and pass the ball with the stick, trying to throw it through a goal to score.

When the Cherokee played, they needed 12 goals to win, but the winning team in a Creek game had to score 20 goals. There could be several hundred players in a game. The game was so rough that players tried to hurt each other. If a woman touched a stick, it could not be used in a game.

Chunkey

Would you like to play your favorite sport all day? When Cherokee boys and men played chunkey, it sometimes lasted that long! Different groups had their own ways of playing. In the Southeast, two players stood side-by-side at the edge of a field. Each player had a spear or wooden pole in his hand. One player threw a stone disc down the field. Each player then ran forward and threw his spear toward where he thought the disc would stop. The player whose spear was closest to the disc—or hit it—won that round. And the game kept on going!

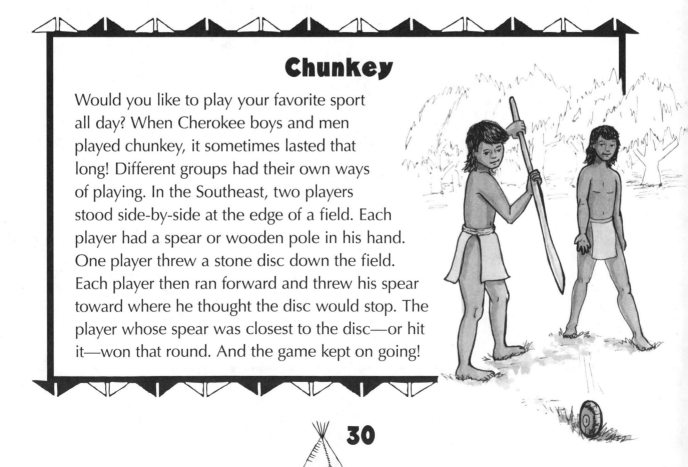

Ceremonies and Festivals

The Southeastern tribes had celebrations just like you do with your family. Their events honored the spirits and tried to make them happy. Because corn was their most important crop, the Green Corn Dance was a big ceremony every year. At the time of the corn harvest, people sang songs, feasted, and danced around a fire in the village square. Above the fire, they hung corn as a way of saying thank you to the spirits for the harvest.

Where Are We Now?

Today, members of the Southeastern tribes live in lots of states, including Florida, Louisiana, Alabama, Texas, and North Carolina. But the largest groups still live in Oklahoma, including 19,000 members of the Seminole Nation, 60,000 members of the Muscogee Creek Nation, and well over 200,000 members of the Cherokee Nation.

In a well-known Seminole story, a clever rabbit attends the Green Corn Dance planning to steal the tribe's fire. After trying many times, he is finally successful and he gives the gift of fire to all Native Americans.

WOW!

In the late 1800s, Cherokee children were sent away to school and allowed to speak only in English. Today, Cherokee children go to schools close to home where they are taught their own language, history, and traditions.

BOOGER MASK

Cherokee warriors danced in a Booger Ceremony the day before a battle. They wore scary masks made from gourds, fur, hornets' nests, or animal hide. Some were painted white with bushy mustaches and opossum hair for eyebrows. Others were painted black with black bear fur for hair. And others were multicolored and had horns or antlers for good luck in hunting. **Ask an adult to help with the scissors.**

1 Cover your workspace with newspaper. Cut off the bottom of the milk jug so you have a "bowl" about 2 inches high (5 centimeters). This will be the mask's base. Cover the base with plastic wrap.

2 Cut the plaster cloth into small pieces. Dip the pieces in the water and lay them on the base. You can make your mask into any character by shaping the pieces of cloth. Leave two eyeholes so you can see out of your mask.

3 Let the mask dry completely. Lift off the base and peel away the plastic wrap. Trim any extra cloth around the edges of the mask. Decorate your mask using paint or markers. Add hair and eyebrows with yarn, feathers, pinecones, and glue.

4 When your mask is dry, use the scissors to poke a hole in either side of the mask. Thread the string through the holes and tie knots to secure it.

SUPPLIES

- newspaper
- plastic 1-gallon milk jug rinsed and dried
- sharp scissors
- plastic wrap
- roll of plaster cloth
- shallow bowl of water
- decorating materials such as paint, yarn, glue, markers, pinecones, feathers
- heavy string

MAKE YOUR OWN

SEMINOLE BEADED NECKLACE

The Seminole loved beads. Women wore necklaces that were about 60 inches long (152 centimeters) and could weigh over 10 pounds (4 kilograms)! They wrapped the necklaces so that none of their neck was showing, and you could only see the beads.

1 Pour even amounts of pasta into your sandwich bags. Use one bag for each color you would like in your necklace. Add a few drops of food coloring and about 1 teaspoon of rubbing alcohol to each bag (5 milliliters).

2 Shake the bag until the pasta is completely coated in dye. Repeat this step with all the bags. Let the mixture sit for 15 to 20 minutes to allow the color to soak in. Pour the contents of each bag onto a separate paper plate and let the pasta dry.

3 Make more beads out of clay. Shape small pieces of clay into balls or other bead shapes, then make a hole with a toothpick in each. Let the beads dry in the sun or air dry over a few days. Paint the beads if you like and let the paint dry.

4 Cut the string into different lengths to make more than one necklace. Try making one 60 inches long (152 centimeters) to feel what the adult Seminole wore.

5 When all the beads are dry, thread them onto the strings in any pattern you'd like. Tie the ends of the string together to complete your necklace.

SUPPLIES

- pasta tubes
- sandwich bags with zip closure
- food coloring
- teaspoon
- rubbing alcohol
- paper plates
- clay
- toothpicks
- paint
- paintbrush
- scissors
- string

33

MAKE YOUR OWN

WOVEN BASKET

The Cherokee wove baskets from pine needles or river cane. They dyed parts of the basket with plant dyes. In this activity you'll make a woven basket from paper.

1 Cut out 11 strips of paper ½ inch wide by 12 inches long from each color of construction paper (1 centimeter by 30 centimeters). Punch a hole at both ends of all the strips.

2 Lay out 11 same-colored strips vertically and parallel to each other. Tape the ends to a table to make weaving easier.

3 Take a strip of the second color and weave it over and under the 11 strips. Try to keep the strips close together.

4 Repeat step 3 with the other 10 strips until you have successfully woven through the square. Remove the tape.

5 Begin with one side. Alternate from right to left and bring the strips into the center of that side. Be certain to line up the holes. Push a straw through the holes. Cut a long piece of yarn for the handle and push it through the straw. Take the straw off and tie a knot to secure the strips.

6 Repeat step 5 on the remaining 3 sides. Gather the yarn in the middle and tie to create a handle. Your basket is ready to hang!

SUPPLIES

- construction paper in two colors
- pencil
- ruler
- scissors
- hole punch
- clear tape
- straw
- yarn

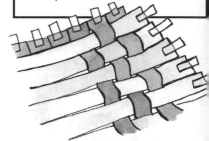

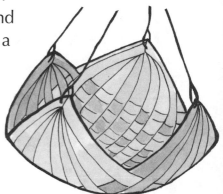

THE SOUTHWEST AND MESOAMERICA

Native Americans of the Southwest lived in what is today Arizona,
New Mexico, Utah, and parts of southern Colorado. The hot,
dry Southwest was home to many tribes. The Apache, Hopi,
Navajo, and Zuni survived by hunting and gathering. The people
in this area were also farmers who grew corn, called maize,
and beans and squash. It was a landscape dominated by the
Grand Canyon, the Colorado River, and the Colorado Plateau.

Words to Know

ANASAZI: a Native American group meaning "the ancient ones." They built huge structures from clay.

PUEBLO: a communal village of stone or adobe homes arranged in levels.

MESA VERDE: an area in the Southwest where Pueblo Indian culture first developed. It is where the corners of Colorado, Utah, Arizona, and New Mexico meet.

DROUGHT: a long period with little or no rain.

The **ANASAZI**, known as the Ancient Pueblo people, were some of the earliest people in the Southwest. They built apartment-like homes in the cliffs. Giant **PUEBLOS** such as the ruins at **MESA VERDE**, in Colorado, had 600 apartments!

Who Are the Pueblo Indians?

Ancient Pueblo village life started around 600 CE in the Mesa Verde region. For about 700 years, the Anasazi lived in the area. They started in small villages and by 1250 CE, there were about 20,000 people living in spectacular dwellings built into the cliffs of what is now Mesa Verde National Park.

But by the 1300s, most of the Anasazi had moved south to join other Pueblo villages in Arizona and New Mexico. They may have left because of a **DROUGHT** that lasted 24 years. No one knows for sure.

36

DESCENDANTS of the Anasazi lived in villages built on top of flat hills called MESAS. The mesas were easy to defend if they were attacked. Because the Spanish word for village or town is "pueblo," these villages became known as pueblos after the Spanish arrived in America. The people came to be known as the Pueblo Indians.

Words to Know

DESCENDANT: the child, grandchild, or later generation of someone who lived earlier.

MESA: a hill with high sides and a flat top.

ADOBE: clay mixed with water and small plant pieces that dries hard.

The Hopi and Zuni who lived in the area built homes, also called pueblos, made of ADOBE bricks. They looked like the homes the Anasazi had built. Adobe bricks are made of clay mixed with grass. The mixture is pressed into a mold, then baked in the hot sun. Drying in the sun bakes them into hard bricks. Pueblos had many units and stood up to five stories high! They had no doors on the first floor. People climbed a ladder to get to the roof and then climbed down a hole into the house. Every night they brought the ladders inside for safety. This is how they locked their doors! Every pueblo had a room built underground called a *kiva*. This is where a family gathered for ceremonies or social events. *Kiva* means "ceremonial room" in the Hopi language.

Not all Southwestern tribes lived in pueblos. The Apache were hunter-gatherers who moved constantly, so they did not have permanent homes. While some Apache lived in tipis, others built round homes called **WIKIUPS**. Women built the frame with wooden poles and tied branches to the frame for walls. The door was a removable animal skin. When the Apache moved to their next camp, they grabbed the poles and left.

The Navajo called themselves Diné or "the people." They lived in an area with trees. They used wood logs to build a cone-shaped home called a **HOGAN**, which they covered with earth.

Traditionally, hogans faced east, with the floor symbolizing Mother Earth and the roof Father Sky. Many Navajo still live in hogans today.

Words to Know

WIKIUP: a dome-shaped home made from branches.

HOGAN: a cone-shaped home built of logs and earth.

Then & Now

Then – The Navajo lived in hogans.

Now – Diné College in Arizona uses the hogan design in their dormitories and their six-story cultural center.

Mesoamerican Cities

Some archaeologists believe the Southwestern tribes were motivated by the Mesoamerican cities of the Maya and the Aztecs to build better towns. The great Maya city of Tikal had pyramids, towers, and tall **STELAE** covered in elaborate designs and **HIEROGLYPHICS**. At its peak, Tikal may have been home to almost 200,000 people. Tikal means "Place of Voices."

Words to Know

STELAE: stone pillars with designs.

HIEROGLYPHICS: a written language that uses pictures and symbols to represent words and ideas.

MANTA: a knee-length cotton dress that fastens over one shoulder.

Clothes

Traditional Pueblo clothing was mostly made from cotton. Pueblo men wore a breechcloth with more material wrapped around their waist. Sometimes they wore leggings underneath to stay warm.

Women wore a dress called a **MANTA** over one shoulder with an embroidered belt. White leggings made of doeskin covered their legs. Just as you may style your hair, Pueblo people did too. Girls fashioned their hair into huge curls above each ear. The curls were made to look like squash blossoms or butterfly wings. Older women wore their hair in simple braids.

Because the Southwest is a huge area, not all tribes wore the same clothing. The Apache and Navajo wore deerskin clothing. Over time, the Navajo learned from their Pueblo neighbors how to make clothes from cotton and wool. Navajo men wore a short blanket-like cape fastened with a belt at the waist. Navajo women wore a long blanket dress called a **BILL**, which was fastened at the waist with a woven belt.

Words to Know

BILL: a dress worn by Navajo women.

Geronimo

Geronimo was a famous Apache warrior originally named Goyathlay or "The One Who Yawns." He was given this name for his easygoing nature. In 1858, after Mexican troops killed his family, he led raids against the Mexicans and the United States. Mexican troops gave him the name Geronimo, though no one knows why. Geronimo has remained a symbol of Native American heritage.

Favorite Foods

No matter where you lived in the Southwest, you hunted wild game and gathered nuts, fruits, and berries. After the Spanish introduced animals such as goats in the 1500s, many tribes kept livestock. Navajo kids just like you helped raise sheep and goats for their milk, meat, and wool.

The Pima and Tohono O'odham, who lived near the Gila River in Arizona, farmed vegetables such as corn and beans. They also gathered desert plants. Every spring, they harvested the fruit of the saguaro cactus. At 70 feet, it's the largest cactus in the United States (20 meters). They used the fruit in their annual Rain Ceremony and turned it into syrup and jam. The ground seeds made a tasty porridge.

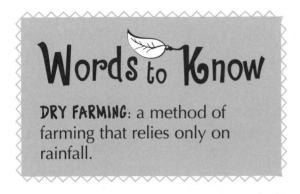

Words to Know

DRY FARMING: a method of farming that relies only on rainfall.

Like their ancient Pueblo ancestors, the Hopi were excellent farmers. But it was very dry where the Hopi lived. They were lucky to get 10 inches of rain in a year (25 centimeters). That's very little water! Of course, they didn't have sprinklers to keep their gardens moist, so the Hopi dug ditches to collect water.

A special planting technique called **DRY FARMING** relies only on rainfall. To give their crops the best chance at a good harvest, the Hopi spaced their plants wide apart and did not plant them too deep in the soil. The Hopi were so good at dry farming they were able to grow corn, melons, peaches, and sunflowers.

The tallest saguaro ever measured reached 78 feet tall (24 meters). The Saguaro cactus is mainly found in southern Arizona near Tucson. You can see many of them at Saguaro National Park.

WOW!

Words to Know

PIKI: a flatbread made from blue corn.

ARTISAN: a skilled worker who makes things by hand.

YUCCA: a root vegetable found in warm parts of the United States and Latin America.

GEOMETRIC: using shapes like lines, circles, or squares.

Would you eat bread that was a gray-green color? One of the Hopi's favorite foods was a flatbread called **PIKI**. The color came from mixing ground blue corn with wood ash and water to make a batter. Bread making was an important skill that mothers taught their daughters.

Southwest Culture

The people of the Southwestern tribes loved creating objects of beauty. Their **ARTISANS** were skilled at basketry, weaving, pottery, and jewelry making. Hopi women made baskets by weaving bundles of fibers from plants such as **YUCCA**. They made colorful dyes from natural sources and wove their colorful fibers in **GEOMETRIC** patterns. Baskets were an important part of Hopi ceremonies and were also used in homes to make and serve food, and even to carry water!

42

Sand Painting

Have you ever created a picture with colored sand? A Navajo medicine man used sand paintings to remove spells the Navajo believed made people ill. The medicine man dyed the sand by mixing pollen, cornmeal, ground charcoal, and powdered minerals. Then he painted on the floor of the sick person's hogan with the sand by letting it drip through his fingers. The sick person sat on the painting and the medicine man chanted. At the end of the ceremony, the medicine man destroyed the picture to get rid of the bad spell.

The Navajo were also great weavers. They spun sheep's wool into yarn that they wove on **LOOMS** into blankets and rugs. It took a weaver about four months to make a rug. No two rugs were alike. Each had its own geometric patterns that included horizontal bands, diamonds, and pictures of animals. According to Hopi and Navajo stories, one of their holy people, Spider Woman, first taught them how to weave.

Words to Know

LOOM: a machine that weaves thread into fabric.

It wasn't long before the Southwest tribes became known for their silver and turquoise jewelry. The Navajo started making silver jewelry in the 1800s by melting silver coins. They punched designs into the silver with nails or **AWLS** and later they learned how to cast shapes in the silver.

Words to Know

AWL: a small pointed tool used to make holes.

Where Are We Now?

Today, the Hopi, Apache, Zuni, and Navajo have reservations in the states of Utah, Arizona, Colorado, and New Mexico. The Navajo Nation (Diné) is the largest Native American tribe in the United States.

Unlike many Native American tribes, the Pueblo Indians were never forced to leave their homelands. Most live in New Mexico and Arizona. People gather at museums, schools, and local festivals to celebrate the culture of the Pueblo people. From May to August each year, there are separate Zuni, Hopi, and Navajo festivals of arts and culture held at the Museum of Northern Arizona.

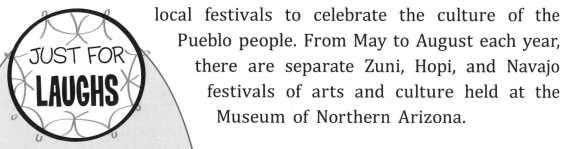

During World War II about 420 Navajos served as Code Talkers so the United States could send secret messages. Their code was never broken.

WOW!

JUST FOR LAUGHS

WHAT DID COACH HAMMER SAY TO THE NAILS BEFORE EVERY GAME?

Everyone give it your awl!

MAKE YOUR OWN

DRY PAINTING

A Navajo medicine man was very important to a Navajo community. People believed that he could communicate with the spirits. A medicine man created sand paintings to be used in ceremonies to help heal people. He created a different picture depending on the bad spell that made each person sick. Each figure in the painting had to be painted in the proper order. In this activity you'll make a painting with cornmeal. What will it look like?

1 Divide the cornmeal equally among the plastic cups.

2 Add just a few drops of food coloring to each cup to make different colors of "sand." Stir well with the spoon.

3 Use the pencil to lightly sketch a picture on the cardboard.

4 When you are happy with your picture, you can begin painting with sand. Cover the section you wish to paint with glue and sprinkle the color of sand you would like over the top. Tap off the excess sand.

5 Repeat step 4 until your entire picture is covered in colored sand.

6 When your sand painting is dry, you can display it.

SUPPLIES

- ⊙ plastic cups
- ⊙ cornmeal
- ⊙ food dyes
- ⊙ spoon
- ⊙ cardboard
- ⊙ pencil
- ⊙ glue
- ⊙ paintbrush

45

KATSINA DOLL

The Hopi carved katsina dolls out of wood that they painted with bright colors. A katsina doll could represent a spirit such as the sun, stars, deer, or hawk. The doll you are going to make can represent anything you choose.

1 Using the scissors, make two slits in the bottom of the Styrofoam ball and push the ball firmly onto the bottle lid.

2 Draw your doll's face on the ball, and add details such as hair with yarn and glue.

3 Wrap a piece of felt around the bottle to make the body of your doll and cut to size. Glue the felt to the bottle.

4 Add additional fabric, feathers, buttons, and beads until you are happy with the way your doll looks.

5 You can display your doll or give it as a gift.

SUPPLIES

- styrofoam ball
- scissors
- small plastic soda bottle with lid
- markers
- yarn
- white glue
- felt
- fabric scraps
- craft feathers, beads, buttons, ribbons, shells

MAYAN GLYPHS

Glyphs are pictures or symbols. The Maya carved symbols into stones to tell stories. Now you can create stories using your own set of glyphs.

1 Write a simple story. It can be about your walk to school, a family tradition, or something you make up.

2 Spread the newspapers over your work surface. Place the foam board on top of the papers.

3 Warm the clay in your hands. Spread the clay evenly over the surface of the foam board. Smooth the surface with your fingertips.

4 Use the sharp end of the paperclip to etch glyphs into the clay to tell your story. See if you can use your symbols more than once. If you make a mistake, smooth over the clay with your fingertips.

5 When you have completed your story, pour the paint onto a paper plate. Press the sponge into the paint and dab the paint lightly all over your clay.

6 When your glyph stone tablet has dried, use it as a guide to telling the story you created.

SUPPLIES

- ⊙ scrap paper
- ⊙ pencil
- ⊙ newspaper
- ⊙ foam board
- ⊙ air-hardening clay
- ⊙ paperclip
- ⊙ gray acrylic paint
- ⊙ paper plate
- ⊙ sponge

THE GREAT PLAINS

Between the Mississippi River and the Rocky Mountains is an area of flat land and rolling hills covered in tall grasses. The Great Plains was home to many Plains tribes including the Blackfoot, Cheyenne, Crow, Comanche, and Sioux.

The Plains was also home to millions of **BISON**. Native Americans hunted bison for food, clothing, shelter, and tools. Every part of the bison was used. **PEMMICAN** was a food made from dried bison meat, berries, and animal fat. Women mixed the ingredients and shaped them into cakes that kept for years! They sewed hides into containers, made horns into spoons, and used the stomach as a cooking pot.

Words to Know

BISON: the correct name for an animal that is commonly called the buffalo.

PEMMICAN: a food made from dried meat, berries, and animal fat.

BUFFALO JUMP: a place where bison herds were chased over a cliff.

NOMADIC: moving from place to place to find food.

A buffalo can run up to 30 miles per hour (50 kilometers per hour). How did the men hunt bison on foot before the Spanish explorers came with horses in the 1500s? One way was to trap bison with a **BUFFALO JUMP**. One group of hunters chased the bison and drove them over the cliff. The hunters waiting below killed the injured buffalo with spears. A cliff in Alberta, Canada, called Head-Smashed-In Buffalo Jump, was used in this way for nearly 6,000 years.

NOMADIC tribes like the Sioux traded bison meat for crops from farming tribes such as the Mandan. People also gathered wild fruit, berries, and prickly pears.

Then & Now

Then = When the Europeans arrived in North America, 60 million bison roamed the Great Plains.

Now = About 200,000 bison live on preserves and ranches.

A Home to Go

The Sioux and the Crow moved frequently in search of food, so they needed homes that could be quickly taken apart. Women could set up a tipi in minutes! First they created the tipi's cone-shaped frame with poles, just like a tent. Then they stretched a cover of tree bark or bison hides over the poles. Some covers were painted with designs from dreams. Finally, the women built a small fire in the center of the tipi for heat. Easy as 1-2-3!

Words to Know

SEMINOMADIC: moving with the seasons to find food, but with a base to plant crops.

SOD: a section of earth with growing grass and roots.

Some Plains tribes, such as the Mandan and the Hidatsa, were **SEMINOMADIC**. Part of the year they lived in tipis and hunted. The rest of the year they lived in villages and farmed.

They built wood frame lodges covered with earth and **SOD**. These protected families from summer heat and bitter winter cold. Lodges had rounded corners, so when they were finished they looked like small hills. In the early 1800s a large Hidatsa town in North Dakota had 130 lodges.

Transportation

Do you travel by car, train, bus, or plane? For thousands of years, walking was the only way to get anywhere on the Plains. But horses changed everything! Horses were used for transportation, hunting, and battle. On horseback, men could keep up with bison and cover distances faster. The Comanche were known for their horsemanship skills. Some Comanche tribes had over 10,000 horses. Imagine the sound of all those hooves!

Words to Know

TRAVOIS: a sled with two poles and a net.

The Cheyenne and the Lakota Sioux used dogs, and later horses, to pull belongings over land on a V-shaped frame called a **TRAVOIS**.

WOW!

The Mandan and Hidatsa lived near rivers. They used small boats shaped like a saucer. The boats were named bull boats for the bison hides that covered the boats' frames. Women made the boats by soaking the hides in water and then stretching them over willow frames. They used a mixture of animal fat and ashes to seal the cracks and seams.

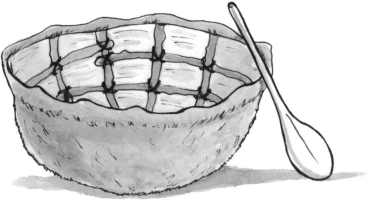

Clothing

Do you buy your clothes at a store? Does your mom sew your clothes? Imagine if she had to make the fabric too! First, men hunted the bison. Then women cleaned and tanned the skins. Tanning was a long process of scraping fur from the skin, then soaking and stretching the skin on a frame many times. This softened the bison hide so the women and girls could make it into clothing.

Women made ankle-length dresses for themselves and aprons or breechcloths for the men and boys. Men wore leather leggings and tunics when the weather turned cool.

Both men and women painted their bodies and faces with paint made from clay or fruit. They had special designs for battles and ceremonies like the Sun Dance. Men pierced their ears and wore long braids decorated with fur, leather, or a feather.

The Plains people used porcupine quills to make designs on their clothes. The designs were so detailed that one war shirt took over a year to decorate. Women dyed the quills and wove them through leather into patterns. Later, they added glass beads brought by the Europeans.

WOW!

Plains tribes are famous for the men's headdresses, especially the war bonnets made of eagle feathers. A warrior had to earn the right to wear each feather by acting with bravery in battle.

Words to Know

SHINNY: a game played with a curved stick and a ball.

Children's Games

Plains children enjoyed games that taught them important skills. Young girls had dolls and toy tipis, and boys had bows and arrows. Everyone enjoyed foot races, string games, and tying bison ribs together to make sleds. **SHINNY** was a popular game using curved wooden sticks and ball. Children played in teams and used their sticks to hit the ball into the other team's goal. Doesn't this sound like hockey?

Sacagawea

Sacagawea was a Shoshone woman who traveled with the explorers Lewis and Clark when they explored the Great Plains, Rocky Mountains, and the Pacific Coast. She and her French-Canadian husband translated for them, showed them shortcuts, and helped them find food.

MAKE YOUR OWN

PLAINS TIPI

The objects of the Native Americans who lived on the Plains were useful and beautiful. Some tipis had decorative symbols on them passed down through families.

1 Peel the bark off your sticks. Lean three sticks against each other so that the narrow ends cross. Join the tops of the poles together with string to form a sturdy tripod.

2 Add the same number of sticks to each side of the tipi frame. The sticks should be evenly spaced out so the tipi frame is strong. Leave a small gap on one side for the door. Tie these sticks together at the top.

3 Loosely wrap a piece of fabric around your tipi frame and cut to size. Do not attach it yet.

4 Lay the fabric out on a flat surface and decorate it with paint.

5 Once the paint has dried, attach your cover by dotting the poles with glue and pressing the fabric to them. Make sure a flap opens for the door.

SUPPLIES

- sticks
- string
- canvas or cotton fabric
- scissors
- fabric paint
- paint brush
- glue

JUST FOR LAUGHS

WHAT TIME IS IT WHEN A BISON SITS ON YOUR TIPI?

Time to get a new tipi.

54

NATIVE AMERICAN SIGN LANGUAGE

Talking to someone from another tribe wasn't easy because each tribe spoke their own language. The Plains people developed a system of hand signals to communicate with other tribes and later with explorers and fur traders. Look at the examples below. Can you think of some ideas that you would like to communicate? Make your own hand signals.

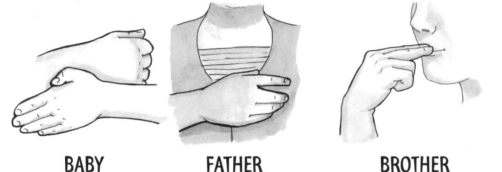

| BABY | FATHER | BROTHER | SON |

Smoke Signals

How did people communicate over long distances without phones, text messages, or email? Have you heard of smoke signals? The person sending a message covered a fire with a blanket and quickly removed it. One puff of smoke meant attention and two puffs meant everything is ok. Three puffs of smoke signaled danger.

MAKE YOUR OWN

PARFLECHE

A parfleche was a container made from bison hide. It was shaped like a large envelope, a tube, or a box. In this project you can make a paper parfleche. **Ask an adult to supervise if you use the Internet.**

SUPPLIES

- ⊙ large paper bag
- ⊙ pencil
- ⊙ ruler
- ⊙ scissors
- ⊙ crayons
- ⊙ hole punch
- ⊙ yarn

1 Measure and cut one large rectangle from the bag, about 12 by 22 inches (30 by 56 centimeters).

2 Fold the long sides in approximately 2½ inches (6 centimeters). Fold the short sides in so they meet in the middle. Press the seams firmly.

3 Unfold the bag. Turn it over and draw authentic Plains Native American designs on the front. Look online or in books for examples.

4 Punch two holes on each of the short flaps about an inch in from the edge (2½ centimeters). Thread one piece of yarn through the holes on one side and another piece of yarn through the holes on the other side.

5 Place an object in the middle of your parfleche. Fold the long sides in, then the short sides. Secure the parfleche by tying the strings, and deliver your package!

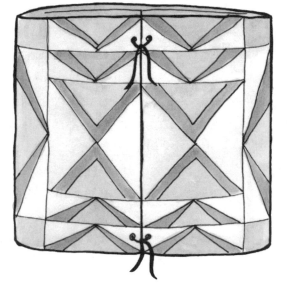

56

SHIELD

A shield made out of bison hide could stop arrows and musket balls. A warrior painted his shield with special symbols such as animals that came to him in a dream.

1 Paint your paper plate and let it dry. Draw an animal such as a bear, bison, or horse on the construction paper. Cut this picture out and glue it to the paper plate to make a shield.

2 Make additional geometric patterns on the construction paper. Cut these shapes out and glue them to your shield.

3 Punch a hole at the bottom of the plate and thread the string through it. Knot the string at the top. Attach feathers and beads to the string and knot the end.

4 Punch one hole at the top of your shield and tie a string through it. Now your shield is ready to hang.

SUPPLIES

- ⊙ paper plate
- ⊙ paint and brush
- ⊙ construction paper
- ⊙ scissors
- ⊙ glue
- ⊙ hole punch
- ⊙ string
- ⊙ feathers and beads

The Battle of Little Big Horn

In 1868, the United States government promised the Black Hills of the Dakota Territory to the Sioux and the Cheyenne. When gold was found in the region, the government wanted the land back. Chiefs Sitting Bull and Crazy Horse led warriors from a group of tribes to defeat the United States army in the Battle of Little Big Horn. The Native Americans were later forced to move to reservations.

57

MAKE YOUR OWN

DECORATIVE CUFFS

Men wore beaded leather cuffs for special occasions or ceremonial dances. Use your own design that makes you feel powerful.

1 Cut a strip of paper that will fit around your wrist. It should be 2½ inches wide (6 centimeters). Repeat this step to make 2 cuffs.

2 Decorate your cuffs with paint and let them dry.

3 Punch 3 holes at both ends of the cuff. Tie yarn to one of the sides. Ask an adult or a friend to tie the cuffs onto your wrists.

SUPPLIES

- construction paper
- scissors
- paint
- paint brush
- hole punch
- yarn

The Winter Count

To record important events, the Lakota drew pictures and symbols of stars, animals, and people on animal skins. The decorated skin was called a winter count. Kids enjoyed listening to their elders retell stories from the winter count at gatherings. This is an important way the tribes passed down their histories through the generations.

THE PACIFIC NORTHWEST

The Pacific Northwest is known for forests of moss-draped trees, snowcapped mountains, and deep INLETS. For thousands of years, the Haida, Chinook, Nuu-chah-nulth, Tsimshian, and Tlingits have called this region home.

The Pacific Northwest Native Americans believed spirits lived in the massive ancient trees surrounding them. Wood from the western red cedar, called the tree of life, was used for bowls, boxes, canoes, clothes, hats, and homes. Before cutting the tree of life, prayers asked permission from the tree's spirit.

59

Words to Know

INLET: a small body of water that leads inland from a larger body of water.

POTLATCH: a ceremony where families gather to celebrate important events.

Northwest tribes lived in villages facing the sea, in longhouses built with western red cedar, spruce, or hemlock. Homes could measure 50 by 60 feet (15 by 18 meters) and stand as tall as a three-story building!

The largest home belonged to the chief. His house could be 100 feet long (30 meters).

WOW!

Sometimes a tribe worked together to build a large home with a living area for each family. But if someone built a house for his own family, it was their own. As each member of a family grew up, married, and had children, they were assigned space in the family house. Does your house get crowded with relatives on holidays? Just imagine if they never left! A longhouse could have one large fire pit or individual family pits to keep the home warm.

60

Chief Maquinna

Chief Maquinna of the Nuu-chah-nulth controlled the fur trade in Nootka Sound, on the west coast of Vancouver Island. In 1803, trade in the area stopped after Chief Maquinna captured and destroyed the trading ship *Boston* because he thought the captain of the ship had insulted him. Chief Maquinna celebrated by hosting the largest **POTLATCH** ceremony anyone had ever seen!

Transportation

The Pacific Ocean bordered the area and massive rivers like the Columbia River sliced through the land. How did these tribes get around? That's right! By boat. Northwestern tribes were able to carve a canoe from a single cedar log. The Haida made prized canoes that sometimes measured as long as 70 feet (21 meters). Try carrying that! It might be easier to lift one of the tiny canoes made for children or the small, two-person canoes used for gathering shellfish or seaweed.

Men set out in huge canoes that could hold up to 60 people to hunt whales, raid other villages, battle in war, or trade with other tribes.

WOW!

Clothing

Can you imagine clothes made from wood? Without buffalo hides to tan, women made clothing from the soft inner bark of cedar trees. Cedar provides great protection from the rain, just like your own raincoat. First the women soaked and boiled the cedar. Then they wove long strips into robes, hats, and capes. They stitched them together using needles made from bird bones and thread from spruce tree roots.

Words to Know

CHILKAT BLANKET: a complex form of weaving passed down by the Chilkat tribe of Alaska.

BUTTON BLANKET: a wool blanket decorated with shell buttons by the Pacific Coast tribes.

The Tlingits wove fancy **CHILKAT BLANKETS**. It could take an entire year to weave one blanket from cedar bark and goat hair. Some were decorated with designs the Tlingits believed could talk. After contact with Europeans, Pacific Northwest tribes traded for wool, cotton, and fur. Haida women turned plain, Hudson Bay Company blankets into ceremonial **BUTTON BLANKETS**. They embroidered them with traditional designs, such as a double-headed eagle, and sewed glass beads or abalone shells around the image.

Hunting and Trapping

In a land of mountains and towering trees that blocked the sun, people could not grow crops. But there was plenty of food in the streams, ocean, and surrounding forests. Beaches were filled with crabs, oysters, and seaweed. Children gathered berries in the forests. Moose and grizzly bears were targets for hunters.

Tribes such as the Makahs and the Nuu-chah-nulth living on Vancouver Island and the Olympic Peninsula were skilled whale hunters. They paddled their strong canoes alongside the whale and one man killed it with his **HARPOON**. A hunt took days, and a whale could tip them over at any time! Being chief harpooner was such an important position that the honor was handed down from father to son.

Words to Know

HARPOON: a weapon with a sharp end that is thrown into an animal's body.

63

As the hunters dragged the dead whale ashore they were welcomed with songs and drumming. After a ceremony to thank the whale, the Northwest tribes used every part of the animal. They ate the meat and used the bones for tools, combs, and knives. **BLUBBER** was eaten and used as oil for candles. Intestines became containers and sinew was used as rope.

Words to Know

BLUBBER: a thick layer of fat under the skin of sea mammals.

SPAWN: to produce eggs or young.

But the most important food for the Northwest people was salmon. A successful salmon catch provided food to last the winter. Millions of salmon make their way from the ocean to **SPAWN** in the rivers and streams where they were born. During spawning, the rivers are so thick with salmon that bears gather to feast in an all-you-can-eat buffet.

A trap called a fishing weir was the most popular way to catch salmon. There were many ways to build a weir, but most weirs looked like a wooden fence made from branches pounded into the ocean floor or riverbed. Fishermen could then strike the trapped salmon with a long spear.

WOW!

The Pacific Northwest

First Salmon Ceremony

Tribes honored the salmon in an annual First Salmon Ceremony. A chief would choose one man to catch the first salmon. Once he returned with the fish, everyone joined to sing songs and say prayers to thank the salmon. The salmon head was placed back in the river facing upstream toward its spawning spot. The rest was cooked and shared. When everyone was done eating, they threw the bones back into the river so the salmon's spirit would find its way home. By honoring the salmon, people believed the harvest would be plentiful and the salmon would return the following year.

Trade

Pacific Northwest tribes had plenty of smoked fish and fish oil to trade for **CARIBOU** hides and birchwood bows. They traded with other coastal tribes and the Inuit to the north and the Cree to the east. But this meant moving goods great distances, east of the Rocky Mountains and the Cascade Range. Tribes like the Tlingits transported goods by canoe and then **SLAVES** hauled the heavy loads from the boat. Slaves were forced to carry loads of 100 pounds (45 kilograms) in baskets strapped to their shoulders and forehead.

Words to Know

CARIBOU: a deer from the Arctic and just south of the Arctic, also called reindeer.

SLAVE: a person owned by another person and forced to work, without pay, against his or her will.

JUST FOR LAUGHS

WHERE DO SALMON KEEP THEIR MONEY?

In a riverbank!

Totem Poles

Have you ever seen a totem pole? The Haida, Tlingits, and Tsimshian carved their family histories into massive cedar poles. There were several types of poles. Some were placed in front of a home, and a hole at the bottom functioned as a doorway into the house! Other poles were carved for sad and happy occasions. Mortuary Totem Poles honored the dead, and Storytelling Totem Poles were made for weddings. Welcome poles greeted people just like a welcome sign today greets people coming to your town or city.

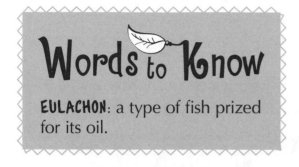

Words to Know

EULACHON: a type of fish prized for its oil.

People put up poles at a potlatch ceremony. Much like your family might celebrate Christmas, Hanukkah, or Kwanzaa with gifts, a potlatch was a gift-giving tradition. It celebrated the birth of a child, marriages, and memorials. To show off his wealth, the host of the potlatch gave away as many gifts as he could, including weapons, blankets, furs, **EULACHON** oil, and even slaves. Sometimes this meant giving away most, if not all, of a family's wealth and belongings. If you're invited to a potlatch, make sure you can carry your gifts home!

TOTEM POLE

Carving a totem pole was an art passed down through generations. The figures on a pole, such as a raven, bear, or frog, told a family's history. What will your totem tell people about you?

1 Poke the straw through the center of the marshmallows. Use between three and five marshmallows.

2 Spread icing on the center of the graham cracker for the base. Press the marshmallow totem into the icing. You may need to put a box behind it until the icing hardens.

3 While your totem is drying, you can work on the wings. Cut a piece of Fruit Roll-Up to resemble wings. Thread a toothpick through the wings and secure it to the back of the totem. You may need to use icing as well.

4 Decorate your pole with the remaining icing and candy.

SUPPLIES

- ⊙ 1 bag of large marshmallows
- ⊙ thin straw
- ⊙ graham cracker
- ⊙ gel icing in various colors
- ⊙ Fruit Roll-Up
- ⊙ assorted candy

In the late 1800s, the potlatch ceremony was made illegal. Most tribes then stopped carving new totem poles, and many poles were cut down or left to rot. The potlatch was made legal again in 1951, and today Northwest Coast tribes raise poles to celebrate important events.

WOW!

MAKE YOUR OWN

BUTTON BLANKET

Haida women sewed designs onto blankets and outlined them with buttons. Traditionally, blankets were made only with the permission of an elder. **Ask an adult to supervise if you use the Internet.**

1 Cut both colors of felt into a rectangle approximately 7½ by 10 inches (19 by 25 centimeters).

2 Look online or in books for traditional Haida designs. Trace your design onto one color of felt with a marker.

3 Cut the design out of the felt and glue it onto the felt piece of the other color.

4 Outline your design with white buttons or glitter.

5 Let your Haida blanket dry before displaying it.

SUPPLIES

- ⊙ red and black crafting felt
- ⊙ scissors
- ⊙ Internet access or library book with Haida designs
- ⊙ marker
- ⊙ white glue
- ⊙ small white buttons or glitter

Native Americans of the Pacific Northwest used dentalium shells as money. These tube-shaped shells look like elephant tusks. The most valuable shells were at least 2½ inches long (5 centimeters). A strand of shells the length of a man's arm could buy a small boat.

WOW!

BASKETRY HAT

The Tlingits wove hats out of cedar or spruce roots. Family symbols often decorated the hats. Design a hat to represent things that are important to your family.

1 Spread newspaper over your work surface. Pour paint onto a paper plate.

2 Place the paper bowl and paper cup upside down on the newspaper. Paint the outsides of both with the brown paint and let it dry.

3 When the paint has dried, use markers to decorate the pieces of your hat with your own family symbols. Glue the opening of the paper cup to the bowl. Let it dry.

4 Attach a string to the bottom of your hat with staples or tape to keep it in place on your head.

SUPPLIES

- ⊙ newspaper
- ⊙ brown paint
- ⊙ paper plate
- ⊙ brush
- ⊙ large paper bowl
- ⊙ large paper cup
- ⊙ assorted markers
- ⊙ glue
- ⊙ tape or stapler
- ⊙ string

Then – Every tribe that fished for salmon had its own form of the First Salmon Ceremony. Hats were an important part of the dress for ceremonies.

Now – Each April, the Celilo Village in Oregon holds a three-day Salmon Ceremony that is open to the public.

MAKE YOUR OWN

BEAR CLAW NECKLACE

Native Americans respected the grizzly bear for its strength. After a bear was killed, a hunter showed its respect for the spirit of the bear by making a necklace using its claws.

1 Take a small piece of clay and form it into a bear claw shape. Place it on your plastic tray. Do this until you have 6 claws.

2 Take your skewer and make a hole at the top of each bear claw for the leather cord to fit through. Allow your bear claws to dry.

3 Paint each bear claw at the tip to make a nail. When the paint has dried, go over each claw with clear nail polish and let it dry.

4 Tie a knot at one end of your necklace and thread on two beads, then a bear claw. Repeat this step until you have added all the bear claws and try your necklace on!

SUPPLIES

⊙ plastic tray
⊙ brown air drying clay
⊙ skewer
⊙ black acrylic paint
⊙ paint brush
⊙ clear nail polish
⊙ leather cord or yarn
⊙ colored wooden beads

Tlingit bear hunters never ate before a hunt. After the hunt, they put the bear's paws and head into the sea or buried them in the ground to honor the bear's spirit.

MAKE A SOFT TWINE BAG

Native Americans living in the Pacific Northwest used soft woven bags to store food and carry personal belongings. Designs were woven into the bag but you will create designs with stamps.

1 Cut two pieces of the burlap into a rectangle 7½ by 10 inches (19 by 25 centimeters).

2 Glue the long sides and bottom of the bag together. Let dry.

3 Make two holes on either side of the top edge for the handle. Thread the twine through the holes and knot to secure.

4 Before painting your bag, sketch out a pattern of different size triangles on the piece of paper. Decide which colors will go in each shape.

5 Pour each paint color onto its own paper plate. Cut the sponges into triangular shapes.

6 Dip a sponge into the paint and press it onto your bag. Continue in this manner to make a design. Allow your bag to dry before using it.

SUPPLIES

- burlap or old feed bag
- scissors
- fabric glue
- twine
- paper and pencil
- paint in various colors
- paper plates
- sponges

Then & Now

Then – In the 1800s, the United States and Canada banned Native American cultural and religious ceremonies. Children were taken from their families and sent to government-run schools.

Now – Today, Pacific Northwest tribes elect their own governments, host celebrations, and run their own schools. They are able to teach their children about the traditions of their culture, including language, clothing, art, and stories.

THE ARCTIC

Imagine living where the average temperature is 22 degrees below zero Fahrenheit in winter (-30 degrees Celsius). The Arctic is a very cold place! In the summer the average temperature is only 32 degrees Fahrenheit (0 degrees Celsius). Archaeologists believe that people have been living in the Arctic for nearly 12,000 years.

The **INUIT** are an Arctic tribe whose name means "the people." They became experts at living in extreme cold by using Arctic animals for food, shelter, clothing, and tools.

 72

Words to Know

INUIT: the native people who live in northern Canada, parts of Greenland, and Alaska.

TUNDRA: a treeless Arctic region that is permanently frozen below the top layer of soil.

DRIFTWOOD: broken pieces of wood that wash up on a beach or riverbank.

IGLOO: a snow hut.

The Algonquin called the people of the far north Eskimos. This means eaters of raw meat. It is a name that is still often used, but these northern groups prefer to use their tribal names.

WOW!

Archaeologists believe that the earliest ancestors of the Inuit lived in northwestern Alaska, along the coast and on the **TUNDRA**. They lived in homes of **DRIFTWOOD** and sod and survived by hunting and fishing. About 1,000 years ago, they began to move east from Alaska to northern Quebec and Labrador in Canada.

Shelter

When you think of an Inuit home, do you think of an **IGLOO**? The Inuit were nomadic hunters who actually built several types of homes. In the summer, Inuit from different areas came together and lived in tents. Because wood was hard to find, they used driftwood or whalebone to build tent frames. Women sewed caribou or seal hides together to make the covering.

Words to Know

QUARMAIT: an Inuit winter home made of sod.

KUDLIK: an Inuit oil lamp.

For the winter, the Inuit built a larger home called a **QUARMAIT** with logs, stone, and sod. This style of home was dug into the ground or hillside for extra warmth. Poles in the ground tilted toward the center were covered with sod blocks and animal skins. Every quarmait had a raised sleeping platform and a small fire pit.

When the Inuit went winter hunting they lived in igloos built with blocks of packed snow. If an igloo was built well, a polar bear could walk across the top and not damage it!

Would you want to sleep on a bed of ice? The Inuit lined ice blocks with furs for sleeping. A **KUDLIK** provided heat and light in the igloo. These shallow stone bowls burned seal or whale oil. As the temperature in the igloo increased, a thin layer of ice formed on the inner wall that helped keep out the cold.

In the Inuit, Aivilik, and Igloolik languages there are 31 words describing snow, including falling snow—*qanniq*, crusty snow—*katakartanaq*, and drinking snow—*aniuk*.

WOW!

74

Clothing

Inuit women told the men what type of fur to bring home for clothing. **WATER RESISTANT** caribou fur was perfect for winter clothing. Lighter but also water-resistant sealskin was used for spring and summer clothing.

WATER RESISTANT: a material that is good at keeping out water.

PARKA: a thick jacket trimmed with fur.

AMAUTI: a woman's parka with an extra-large hood.

During the winter, Inuit wore **PARKAS** of caribou skin. Parkas had an inner layer of fur facing the body, and an outer layer with the fur facing out. A woman carried her child in the large hood of an **AMAUTI** parka, which kept her hands free to work.

Who Turned Out the Lights?

When you think of Arctic clothing, do you think of sunglasses? Eye protection was very important in the Arctic because of all the snow. White reflects everything. Without their snow goggles made from caribou antlers and walrus tusks, the Inuit could go blind from the strong glare of the Arctic sun on the snow.

Everyone wore soft boots of caribou or seal skin called **KAMIKS**. There were no tape measures, so women used their hands and fingers to measure someone's feet before sewing their boots. Inuit kamiks were works of art decorated with fancy stitches, animal fur, and feathers.

Words to Know

KAMIKS: boots made of animal skin, also called mukluks.

UMIAK: a large, skin-covered boat.

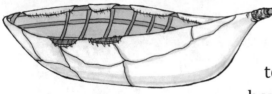

Hunting

The Inuit hunted large animals on land and in the sea. The bowhead whale was an important part of Inuit life. It could only be hunted in the summer once the thick Arctic ice began to break up. When the bowhead came to feed, a whaling captain planned the hunt. He led hunters in a large boat called an **UMIAK**.

Once the Inuit began trading with European fishermen and whalers, many died of new diseases. They caught smallpox, tuberculosis, and measles from the Europeans.

WOW!

One hunter waited with a harpoon for the whale to surface. The harpoon had sealskin bags filled with air attached to it. The sealskin bags slowed the whale down and stopped it from diving deeper. Harpooning might sound cruel to you, but it was a matter of survival for the Inuit. One whale fed a whole community for the winter.

Words to Know

LEGEND: an ancient story that may or may not have really happened.

INUKSUK: a stone landmark used in the Arctic.

When the water froze over, the Inuit moved out onto the ice to hunt seals. A hunter placed a feather or a wood chip into the water of a seal's breathing hole. Then he waited and watched, sometimes for hours. When the object moved, the hunter knew a seal was coming up to breathe and he got ready to lunge at it with his harpoon.

The Caribou

If you read Inuit **LEGENDS**, you'll understand the importance of caribou in their culture. One legend tells of a man who cut a deep hole into the earth and wished for a caribou. Soon enough caribou came from this hole to feed everyone. The Inuit hunted caribou at the end of the summer when they gathered to migrate south to their wintering grounds.

A huge stone marker called an **INUKSUK** played an important role in the caribou hunt. An inuksuk was used for communication among hunters. The traditional meaning is "you are on the right path." An inuksuk looks like a giant person with its arms out wide. When hunters had luck finding caribou in a certain location, they would place antlers on top of an inuksuk to let other hunters know.

The Inuit believed everything had a spirit. The most important spirit was Sedna, who protected sea mammals. The Inuit believed Sedna only let them eat her sea creatures if she was shown respect. After a hunter killed a seal, he dropped melted snow into the seal's mouth to thank Sedna for giving him food.

Mythology

What's white, weighs up to 1,700 pounds (771 kilograms), and can stand 8 to 10 feet tall (2 to 3 meters)? The wise polar bear played an important role in Inuit **MYTHS**. In their stories, polar bears taught the Inuit how to hunt for seals.

In one well-known myth, a polar bear tries to escape four hunters and their dogs by running into the sky. The hunters and their dogs followed. One hunter returns to Earth to retrieve his dropped mitt. The other hunters, their dogs, and the polar bear never returned.

Instead, they became part of the group of stars you might know called the Big Dipper. The bowl part of the dipper is the bear and the stars that form the handle are the hunters chasing it.

Words to Know

MYTH: a traditional story dealing with ancestors or heroes that explains something.

Transportation

Can you imagine how difficult it was for the Inuit to hunt sea creatures before engines were invented? They used their own power to paddle a boat called a **KAYAK**. Kayaks were long and narrow with a wooden or bone frame covered with seal or caribou skin. Men powered the boat with a long paddle. When a kayak was not being used, the Inuit stored it up high so their dogs wouldn't chew the skin!

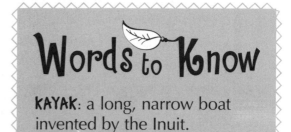

Words to Know

KAYAK: a long, narrow boat invented by the Inuit.

AMULET: a small piece of jewelry worn as protection against evil.

SOAPSTONE: a soft stone.

They also hunted whales and walruses in umiaks. These deep, wide boats could hold over 30 people plus supplies! It took a lot of teamwork to row an umiak, so people sang songs as they rowed to keep in time. Today, umiaks used in northern communities are powered by motors.

Carving

The Inuit have been carving tools, lamps, and **AMULETS** from animal horns, bones, and tusks for thousands of years. They also carved small religious figures they believed brought hunters luck and kept evil spirits away. Today the Inuit do some of their carving out of **SOAPSTONE** and other more commonly found stones such as serpentine.

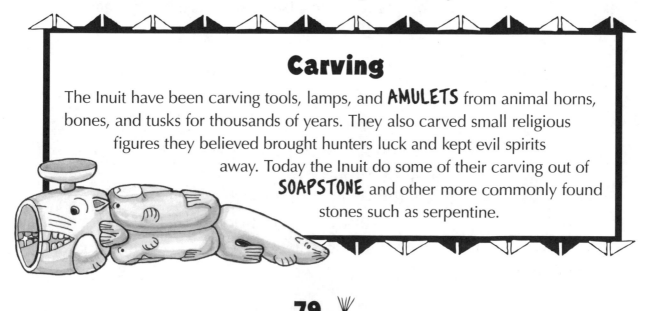

Eskimo Dogs

In the Arctic people traveled on sleds pulled by Eskimo dogs called huskies. The strongest dogs could pull almost 200 pounds (90 kilograms). That's as much as you and a couple of friends! The dogs also sniffed out seal holes for hunters.

School and Games

Traditionally, Inuit children didn't go to school. They learned from their parents. Boys learned to hunt and build shelters and girls learned to make clothes and prepare meals. But they still had time for fun with toys like seal skin balls and skipping ropes. Do you ever play cat's cradle with string? They also enjoyed wrapping sinew around their fingers to make shapes. Sinew was also used to create characters from stories.

Men played wrestling and kicking games that kept them fit and strong. In the one-foot high kick, the player had to kick a hanging target and land on the same leg. The player who kicked the highest target was the winner. Maybe you can try the sport at the Arctic Winter Games. This celebration of traditional northern sports and culture is held every two years.

INUKSUK DISPLAY

An inuksuk was an important tool for survival in harsh Arctic winters. Try making more than one inuksuk using different types of rocks. You can also try balancing your rocks and making an upright structure instead of gluing them down flat. **Ask an adult for help with the hot glue gun.**

SUPPLIES

- cardboard
- ruler
- scissors
- variety of flat rocks
- hot glue
- black shadow box 8 by 10 inches (20 by 25½ centimeters) (optional)

1 Measure a piece of cardboard 8 x 10 inches (20 x 25½ centimeters) and cut it out.

2 Gather your rocks and explore different ways to build your inuksuk. Take your time and move them around until you have a shape you like.

3 With an adult's help, glue the rocks to the cardboard.

4 If you'd like, you can display your inuksuk in a shadow box. They look great on the wall in a black box!

JUST FOR **LAUGHS**

WHAT ARE THE BEST BURGERS GRILLED IN THE ARCTIC?

Icebergers!

Today, the inuksuk is used on the Nunavut flag. It was the logo of the 2010 Vancouver Winter Olympics.

WOW!

81

INUIT TUG-O-WAR

This Inuit version of tug-o-war requires two players to sit on the ground facing each other.

1 Two players sit on the ground with their legs slightly apart and feet touching. The players hold onto the stick.

2 Next, ask an adult to count. On the count of 3, each player begins pulling the stick. The winner is the one who lifts the other player off the ground.

SUPPLIES

- ⊙ long stick or yard (meter) stick
- ⊙ two players

SKY WATCHING

On a clear night, go outside and see if you can locate the Great Bear or the Ursa Major constellation. In North America you usually have to look in the northern sky to spot this constellation. An easy way to find it is to locate a group of stars known as the Big Dipper within Ursa Major. The bowl part of the dipper is the bear in the Inuit legend. The stars that form the handle are the hunters chasing it.

INUIT SCULPTURE

In Inuit art today, sculptures often show Arctic birds, land animals such as polar bears, and sea mammals such as whales or seals. Now you can make your own from a block of soap. **Have an adult help you with the knife and vegetable peeler.**

SUPPLIES

- paper
- pencil
- newspaper
- soft bar of soap such as Dove
- butter knife
- vegetable peeler
- glass of water
- toothpicks or wooden skewer

1 Decide which animal you are going to carve. Start by sketching the animal on a piece of paper.

2 Spread the newspaper on your work surface. Place the bar of soap on the newspaper. Begin by carving the general shape of the animal out of your soap. Only remove small pieces at a time. Try using the knife and the vegetable peeler and see what works better for you. Dipping the tools into a glass of water makes it easier.

3 Use the toothpick or skewer to add small details such as eyes, fur, or scales.

4 When your piece is finished, smooth it out with your fingertips.

5 Use any extra soap scraps to build up texture and features by molding them and pressing them into the body of the animal. Now your sculpture is ready to be displayed.

Seal hunters used a tool called a seal call, which looked like a short rake. A hunter used it to scratch the ice. It made a sound like a seal so other seals would come looking.

WOW!

MAKE YOUR OWN

NATIVE AMERICAN CULTURES MADLIB

If you like word games, then you'll enjoy this activity! Photocopy this page and fill in the blank lines with words from the glossary or text of this book. When you finish, read your story aloud.

noun: a person, place, or thing
plural noun: more than one noun
adjective: a word that modifies a noun (a <u>red</u> balloon)
verb: an action word
adverb: a word that modifies a verb (I walked <u>slowly</u>)

_____ had to pass two tests before being accepted into the great
<small>YOUR NAME</small>
tribe of the _____ who lived in the _____. You are allowed
<small>NOUN</small>   <small>NOUN</small>
to bring _____ and _____ on the challenge.
<small>NOUN</small>   <small>NOUN</small>

For the first test, you must build a _____ _____ from _____,
<small>ADJECTIVE</small>   <small>NOUN</small>   <small>NOUN</small>
_____, and _____. Amazingly, you build it in only _____days.
<small>NOUN</small>   <small>NOUN</small>   <small>NUMBER</small>

For the next test you must find _____and _____ in the _____.
<small>NOUN</small>   <small>NOUN</small>   <small>NOUN</small>
You search and search but can only find _____ and _____.
<small>NOUN</small>   <small>NOUN</small>

On the way back to camp you run into fierce _____. And have to _____
<small>PLURAL NOUN</small>   <small>VERB</small>
_____ all the way to a _____. It is a _____ _____
<small>ADVERB</small>   <small>NOUN</small>   <small>ADJECTIVE</small>   <small>NOUN</small>
night. You think that you hear a _____ and see a _____.
<small>NOUN</small>   <small>NOUN</small>

In the morning, you run into the _____ who take you captive and bring you to
<small>PLURAL NOUN</small>
their _____. Eventually they trust you with _____ and you become a
<small>NOUN</small>   <small>NOUN</small>
_____ with a _____ and a _____.
<small>NOUN</small>   <small>NOUN</small>   <small>NOUN</small>

And you live happily ever after.

Glossary

ADOBE: clay mixed with water and small plant pieces that dries hard.

AMAUTI: a woman's parka with an extra-large hood.

AMULET: a small piece of jewelry worn as protection against evil.

ANASAZI: a Native American group meaning "the ancient ones." They built huge structures from clay.

ANCESTOR: someone from your family or culture who lived before you.

APRON: a panel worn over the front and back of a belt.

ARCHAEOLOGIST: a scientist who studies ancient people and their cultures by looking at what they left behind.

ARCHITECTURE: the style or look of a building.

ARCTIC: the region in the far north around the North Pole.

ARTISAN: a skilled worker who makes things by hand.

ASI: a Cherokee winter home built with branches and mud.

AWL: a small pointed tool used to make holes.

BERING STRAIT: a narrow sea passage between Russia in Asia and Alaska in North America.

BILL: a dress worn by Navajo women.

BISON: the correct name for an animal that is commonly called the buffalo.

BLUBBER: a thick layer of fat under the skin of sea mammals.

BREECHCLOTH: a single piece of cloth wrapped around the hips.

BUFFALO JUMP: a place where bison herds were chased over a cliff.

BUTTON BLANKET: a wool blanket decorated with shell buttons by the Pacific Coast tribes.

CALICO: a cotton fabric.

CANOE: a narrow boat with pointy ends.

CARIBOU: a deer from the Arctic and just south of the Arctic, also called reindeer.

CHICKEE: a Seminole home built with plant materials in the swamps of Florida.

CHILKAT BLANKET: a complex form of weaving passed down by the Chilkat tribe of Alaska.

CLAN: a family group related through a common ancestor.

COMMUNITY: a group of people who live in the same area.

CONSTELLATION: a group of stars that form a picture.

CROP: plants grown for food and other uses.

CULTURE: the beliefs and way of life of a group of people.

CUSTOMS: traditions or ways of doing things, such as dress, food, or holidays.

DESCENDANT: the child, grandchild, or later generation of someone who lived earlier.

DRIFTWOOD: broken pieces of wood that wash up on a beach or riverbank.

DROUGHT: a long period with little or no rain.

DRY FARMING: a method of farming that relies only on rainfall.

EULACHON: a type of fish prized for its oil.

FERTILE: land that is good for growing crops.

GENERATION: all the people born around the same time.

GEOMETRIC: using shapes like lines, circles, or squares.

GLACIER: a huge sheet of ice and snow.

GREAT LAW OF PEACE: the spoken rules that bound the Iroquois tribes together.

GREAT PLAINS: a flat area of land that is covered with grass in the middle of North America.

HARPOON: a weapon with a sharp end that is thrown into an animal's body.

HEPTAGON: a shape with seven sides.

HERITAGE: the art, buildings, traditions, and beliefs that are important to the world's history.

HIAWATHA: the leader and founder of the Iroquois Confederacy.

HIDE: an animal skin.

HIEROGLYPHICS: a written language that uses pictures and symbols to represent words and ideas.

HOGAN: a cone-shaped home built of logs and earth.

ICE AGE: a period of time when ice covers a large part of the earth.

IGLOO: a snow hut.

INLET: a small body of water that leads inland from a larger body of water.

INUIT: the native people who live in northern Canada, parts of Greenland, and Alaska.

INUKSUK: a stone landmark used in the Arctic.

KAMIKS: boots made of animal skin, also called mukluks.

KAYAK: a long, narrow boat invented by the Inuit.

KUDLIK: an Inuit oil lamp.

LAND BRIDGE: a connection between two land masses that allows humans and animals to settle in new areas.

LEGEND: an ancient story that may or may not have really happened.

LIVESTOCK: animals raised for food and other uses.

LONGHOUSE: a long home that housed several Iroquois families.

LOOM: a machine that weaves thread into fabric.

MANTA: a knee-length cotton dress that fastens over one shoulder.

MESA: a hill with high sides and a flat top.

MESA VERDE: an area in the Southwest where Pueblo Indian culture first developed. It is where the corners of Colorado, Utah, Arizona, and New Mexico meet.

MESOAMERICA: the region that includes parts of Mexico and Central America.

MIGRATE: to move from one place to another when seasons change.

MOCCASIN: a shoe made from soft leather.

MYTH: a traditional story dealing with ancestors or heroes that explains something.

NATURAL RESOURCE: something found in nature that is useful to humans, such as water to drink, trees to burn and build with, and fish to eat.

NOMADIC: moving from place to place to find food.

PALISADE: a fence made of rows of pointed posts.

PARKA: a thick jacket trimmed with fur.

PEMMICAN: a food made from dried meat, berries, and animal fat.

PIKI: a flatbread made from blue corn.

PILGRIMS: people who came from England in the 1620s to settle in Massachusetts.

PORTAGE: to carry a boat over land.

POTLATCH: a ceremony where families gather to celebrate important events.

PUBERTY: the stage of development when a child's body starts to change into an adult body.

PUEBLO: a communal village of stone or adobe homes arranged in levels.

QUARMAIT: an Inuit winter home made of sod.

RAWHIDE: animal skin that has not been turned into leather.

REPRESENTATIVE: a single person who speaks for the wishes of a group.

RESERVATION: land owned by the United States but set aside for Native American tribes. There are about 326 Indian reservations in the United States.

SAP: the liquid that flows in maple trees and other plants.

SEMINOMADIC: moving with the seasons to find food, but with a base to plant crops.

SHINNY: a game played with a curved stick and a ball.

SINEW: a strong band of animal tissue that connects muscles to bones.

SLAVE: a person owned by another person and forced to work, without pay, against his or her will.

SNOWSHOE: a shoe like a tennis racket worn on each foot for walking in deep snow.

SOAPSTONE: a soft stone.

SOD: a section of earth with growing grass and roots.

SPAWN: to produce eggs or young.

STELAE: stone pillars with designs.

TANNING: the process of turning an animal skin into leather by soaking it in liquid.

THATCH: straw or leaves used as a roof.

TOBOGGAN: a long, narrow sled.

TRADE: to exchange goods for other goods or money.

TRAVOIS: a sled with two poles and a net.

TRIBE: a large group of people with common ancestors and customs.

TUNDRA: a treeless Arctic region that is permanently frozen below the top layer of soil.

TUNIC: a long, loose-fitting shirt.

UMIAK: a large, skin-covered boat.

WAMPUM: shell beads used in ceremonies or to trade.

WARRIOR: a brave fighter.

WATER RESISTANT: a material that is good at keeping out water.

WIGWAM: the rounded or rectangular homes of the Algonquin tribes. Cone-shaped wigwams are different from tipis mainly because they are fixed and not portable.

WIKIUP: a dome-shaped home made from branches.

YUCCA: a root vegetable found in warm parts of the United States and Latin America.

Web Sites

American Indians of the Pacific Northwest Collections:
content.lib.washington.edu/aipnw/

Bureau of Indian Affairs:
www.bia.gov/

Discovery Education—Native American History:
www.discoveryeducation.com/teachers/free-lesson-
plans/native-american-history.cfm

National Geographic Kids—Native American Photographs:
kids.nationalgeographic.com/kids/photos/native-americans/

PBS We Shall Remain:
www.pbs.org/wgbh/amex/weshallremain/

PBS—The Living Edens: Arctic Oasis:
www.pbs.org/wnet/nature/arcticoasis/index.html

Library of Congress Native Americans:
www.loc.gov/teachers/classroommaterials/themes/native-americans/index.html

Library of Congress—Indians of North Americas:
www.loc.gov/rr/main/indians_rec_links/overview.html

Library of Congress—Images of Indians of North America:
www.loc.gov/rr/print/coll/232_naov.html

Edward S. Curtis—The North American Indian:
memory.loc.gov/ammem/award98/ienhtml/curthome.html

**Smithsonian National Museum of Natural History
online exhibit of Lakota Winter Counts**:
wintercounts.si.edu

University of Washington—Native American History:
www.lib.washington.edu/subject/history/tm/native.html

Go to nomadpress.net
to see other resources and
a list of museums to visit.

JUST FOR LAUGHS

**WHAT IS AT THE END OF
THE NORTH POLE?**

The letter E.

Index